Quakerism
IN THE CITY OF NEW YORK
1657-1930

Quakerism in the City of New York 1657–1930

John Cox, Jr.

HERITAGE BOOKS
2011

HERITAGE BOOKS
AN IMPRINT OF HERITAGE BOOKS, INC.

Books, CDs, and more—Worldwide

For our listing of thousands of titles see our website
at
www.HeritageBooks.com

A Facsimile Reprint
Published 2011 by
HERITAGE BOOKS, INC.
Publishing Division
100 Railroad Ave. #104
Westminster, Maryland 21157

Originally published:
Press of Henry W. Dutton & Son
90 & 92 Washington Street
Boston, Massachusetts
1869

— Publisher's Notice —
In reprints such as this, it is often not possible to remove blemishes from the original. We feel the contents of this book warrant its reissue despite these blemishes and hope you will agree and read it with pleasure.

International Standard Book Numbers
Paperbound: 978-0-7884-1560-9
Clothbound: 978-0-7884-8624-1

Contents

	PAGE
Foreword	ix
Preface	xi
Introductory	3
The Genesis: 1657	8
"First Publishers of the Truth"	20
The Meeting for Worship	22
Meeting Houses	28
Concerns of the Meeting	39
Philanthropy and Charity	42
Negroes and Slavery	54
Peace and War	71
Intoxicants	84
Marriage	86
Music and the Drama	94
Administration of Discipline	97
"If Differences Arise"	104
Language	106
Moderation and Plainness	108
Equality of the Sexes	110
Quakers in Civil and Public Life	113

CONTENTS

	PAGE
Quaker Doctors	146
Quakers in Other Professions	159
Education	161
The Public School System	176
The Monthly Meeting: Its Habitat; Its Business Methods	184
The Preparative Meetings	187
The Records	189
Cemeteries	194
The Separation of 1828	198
"The Conclusion of the Whole Matter"	202
Appendix	205
Index	211

Illustrations

    PAGE

English ketch, "*Quaiche Angloise servant pour le commerce*," from Gueroule's engravings of ships of the Mediterranean and of the Ocean. The *Woodhouse* was very probably of this type 8

View of New Amsterdam, from Vischer's map, 1651-1654 10

Stadt Huys, at Coenties Slip, 1642 to 1690, from Valentine's Manual 14

Deed for land for first Meeting House, 1696 (text on p. 207) 30

The first Meeting House, built 1697, and other N. Y. churches, from the margin of David Grimm's map of New York, 1742-1744 . 32

Address to the Governor, 1672 . . . 72

A Black Ball Liner, 1826, from a painting by Charles Robert Patterson, by permission. The black disk on foresail does not appear in this reproduction 134

Earliest Quaker minute in America . . . 190

Foreword

In a great crisis of American history Patrick Henry declared: "I have but one lamp by which my feet are guided and that is the lamp of experience; I know no way of judging the future but by the past." Admitting the truth of this saying, we recognize the value of written history. Religious history in particular is worth while at the present time. Never, perhaps, has religious thinking undergone such rapid changes as in the past generation, and the prospect is for further change. If the religious landmarks of the past can serve to any degree as guideposts for the future, they are indeed worthy of preservation.

Fortunately for the Society of Friends, its history has never been neglected. George Fox, who founded the Society, also laid the foundations for its history in the Journals of his life. A goodly group of his followers provided abundant historical material in their generous output of controversial literature. William Sewel, Joseph Besse, and Robert Proud added their great contributions in the eighteenth century. In our own day there has been a veritable outpouring of Quaker history and biography, culminating in that great general history of Friends, the Rowntree Series, by William C. Braithwaite, Rufus M. Jones, and their associates. No one who reads these works and knows present-day Quakerism can escape the conviction that "the roots of the present lie deep in the past."

Titles concerning local history are by no means lacking from the Quaker book-shelf. There are not a few accounts in print of Friends' settlements, meetings, and meeting-houses. Now comes, appropriately, the history of Friends and Friendly activities in the greatest metropolitan area of America. The present volume tells the story of the Quakers from their arrival in quaint New Amsterdam to their activities in ultra-modern New York. Fortunately it could be written by one who has long been familiar with the basic manuscript records of New York Quakerism. For many years the author has labored for a closer cooperation between the two great branches of American Friends. Hence he views the facts of Quaker history with unbiased discrimination and a broad charity. For reference purposes the book will be useful to all those interested in Quakerism or in religious history. The chapters on the philanthropic and reform interests of Friends are not without significance as part of the history of the United States. The book is well worth reading and keeping.

RAYNER W. KELSEY.

Haverford, Pennsylvania,
Eighth Month, 25th, 1930.

Preface

This volume is offered as a contribution to the religious history of New York City. The hasty observer might judge, from the gay and careless throng which nightly seeks pleasure in the lights of Broadway, that there can be little religion or religious history here. The philosophic mind must however see that now, and through all the city's history, Jew and Christian, Quaker and Romanist, have had one common aim—the growth and development of the individual soul, largely through sacrifice of self for others; must see how all systems of religion may become encrusted with form, or creed, or ritual, and to what sad damage; and haply may know what liberation of thought, what joy of spirit and enlivened purpose comes to those who can cut through the dead crust to the real Life obscured by it. The thinker must also see that the agencies for spiritual and cultural development in which this city ranks high—its churches, libraries, colleges; its hospitals and charities—are the result of a spirit in man which is indomitably desirous of good, and of subduing evil. Matthew Arnold called this the "force which makes for righteousness"; George Fox proclaimed it to be "that of God in all men."

The author has no hope or desire that all should believe alike, even among Quakers, but has the firm conviction that the "two and seventy jarring sects," having a common purpose should display a common charity and an inclusive love.

This volume is an attempt to tell the story of one of these religious organizations, and its part in the city's history, and with Bacon, "to save and recover somewhat from the deluge of time." It might have been told in more words, but the reason for condensing it may be shown in the following quotation from William Sewel's preface to his *History of the Quakers*, 1722:

"It hath not been for want of Matter that this History hath not run out farther, since I could have made it thrice as big, if I had been minded so to do. . . . I would not glut my Reader with many Things of one and the same Nature; but have endeavoured by Variety of Matter, to quicken his Appetite; and therefore have intermixt the serious Part sometimes with a facetious Accident."

JOHN COX, JR.

Chappaqua, N. Y.
Ninth Month, 12th, 1930.

Quakerism
IN THE CITY OF NEW YORK
1657-1930

Introductory

Quakerism in the City of New York inherits, and is, the result of over two and a half centuries of corporate existence. It is to-day, as an organic entity, the net outcome of all its past—of high ideals, of heroic sacrifices, and, alas! of low failures. It is permanently endowed by the inspiring example of many saintly lives, and it still shows the scars of suffering from that fateful lack of love which we call the "Separation." Its inner history as a vital force for righteousness in the individual, the community and the world, may be faintly discerned by the thoughtful student. The entire effect of its influence toward a higher life and nobler civilization may only be glimpsed, and cannot wholly be estimated.

It is well for those who are Quakers to pause for an hour in the hurried life of to-day to consider their past, that they may more worthily bear their part in the present and that they may better hold themselves in readiness for whatever future is to be theirs. It may be well for those not of this faith to learn somewhat of the causes and effects of its existence in this city.

The inventions of yesterday are so embedded in our consciousness; the countless adjuncts and results of civilization which make the life of the poorest laborer richer and safer than that of the nobility of the seventeenth century; all these are so much a matter of course with us that it is only with an effort that we can visualize the past. Tea and coffee were little known in the colony, wheaten bread a rare delight, garden vegetables few and coarse, and the fireplace with its crane, hook and trammel the sole cooking contrivance. So much for food. As for clothing, the cordwainer came to each family in turn to make the "shoon," and the good housewife made all else from the sheared wool and the broken flax. Then, a letter, carried by the good nature of a sea captain or traveler or the kindness of a friend, might eventually reach its destination; to-day our regular Air Mail spans the continent in thirty hours. We may imagine such a time as differing less from the age of Troy than from our own. In some ways, yes. But in the one vital particular of thought, far removed from their own past and more nearly allied to us. For with all its superstition, lack of general education and cruelty of laws, the seventeenth century was definitely aligned with the future, and turned from the past. Each community was then largely self contained; now, from the time we eat our breakfast fruit from California to the time we lie us down to sleep under blankets of Argentine wool, we are dependent on the whole world. It requires the care and labor of a thousand men to produce our daily loaf of bread. Our forefathers and foremothers came slowly to meeting on pillioned horses or in ox-drawn carts; to-day we are quickly brought in luxury by cunning engines propelled by strange vapors—all wholly unimaginable to those earnest souls whose steadfastness aforetime laid the foundation on which we live in ease. But certain things have not changed; least of all the need of the human soul to commune with the Divine, the need of quietude of spirit and calmness of judgment, poise. The meeting gathers to-day under the same sheltering spirit, in the same living silence, as did those in the bright morning of Quakerism—as indeed must all Quaker meetings if they are to have Life and Power.

In 1644, George Fox, son of a Leicestershire weaver, came to the realization, in the full sense of that word, that God dwells in the heart of every man. To the youth of twenty this flaming reality, this eternal verity, came as a new discovery. "All the earth had a new smell to me." Man became in very truth the Temple of God; he cannot be born in sin, and needs neither priest nor ritual to restore him from sin or to bring him into communion with his loving Creator. This radically new faith of the Immanence of Divinity in Humanity revealed to Fox that all one's fellow men are brothers and equally loved of God. To those afflicted with disease, poverty or vice, help must be given. On the other hand, Kings, Judges, Bishops, Justices or other officials were to be met with covered head and unbended knee. Reverence and obeisance were to be rendered alone to God. Fox realized that our loving Father speaks to all now, as he did to the prophets of old. Worship should therefore include periods of silence, that communion may be free and full. Elegance and vain display in dress, pride of place or power, the intemperate use of any thing, are distractions which tend to separate us from God, hence are to be shunned. Gambling, being based on a desire to acquire gain without a fair return, weakens the character.

This faith was not negative; it did not make for gloom, but rather for light and joy; for a virile, forthright life, filled with the ardor which Fox and his nearest followers exhibited. If the Quaker home lacked music and ornament—as did the Presbyterian and Independent homes—it had the special realization of the eternal love of God, and inspired a love of all mankind, and of the beast creation which serves mankind. In such a home children were welcomed, not as sinners by birth, but as undeveloped characters, to be made strong and fine. This liberating faith has resulted in a radically different principle of instruction in Quaker schools. Training of character is the vital matter, in which George Fox would include "all that is civil and useful in creation."

The followers of a great leader ever tend to a worship of the leader; to greater devotion to his application of principles than to the cause and source of them. The simplicity of Fox in wearing plain clothing (at one period the leathern breeches and jerkin of the common laborer) caused his immediate followers to remove gold braid, lace and other ornaments from their attire. A few generations and the Quaker costume with which we are familiar became as fixed, in style and color, as the Median law. The democracy inherent in the Quaker faith could not adopt the newly imported Continental fashion of addressing "superiors" with the plural pronoun, as this separated into classes the equal children of God. The language absorbed and digested this change of structure to the degree that the plural pronoun is now used by all, and carries no inference of superiority. The "plain language" is retained by Friends only as a language of affection, in the family or among close friends.

How the Society in this city suffered spiritual loss, while increasing the codification of its organic discipline; how, grown strong, but not sufficiently mindful of "that of God in them" it suffered the tragedy of a Separation; and what it has been and done through the years, I have undertaken to tell. Much of it can be told only in terms of individual effort, hence many individuals are named.

The Genesis: 1657

The Dutch were settled securely, as they thought, in New Netherland. Their last and strongest Director-General was at the height of his power, and at the beginning of his most difficult problem—the encroachment of the English. Rhode Island had been a haven of religious liberty for twenty years, but the other settlements of New England were intent mainly on liberty to prevent disagreement with or variance from their kind of religious government. For they were theocracies. They had been disturbed the previous year by members of a new sect, whose doctrines tended to the destruction of theocracies. Boston had sent off home to England, bag and baggage, the few Quaker preachers who had come, and was presently to whip disturbers of that sort for a first visit, and to hang them for a second coming. Quakers had spread over England, had appeared in Ireland, in France, in Holland, in Barbados, in Jerusalem.

So in 1657 the Quakers came again. They saw all the clearer the need of softening the hard hearts of New England, and in their earnest faith and forthright zeal they knew not fear. But no ship would carry them, as its master would suffer a grievous fine

English Ketch, 17th century
The *Woodhouse* was probably of this type

for transporting a Quaker to Boston. Robert Fowler, who had just built himself the *Woodhouse* for a coasting vessel, says in his *True Relation,* "This vessel was appointed for this service from the beginning, as I have often had it manifested unto me; that it was said within me several times, 'Thou hast her not for nothing'; and also New England presented itself before me." So Robert, with his little coasting vessel, was ready to carry other Quakers to Boston. The voyage took two whole months, and, lacking wireless, lacking equally the sextant, lacking even a compass of much accuracy, instead of Boston they reached New Amsterdam, entering through the Sound and Hell Gate. They anchored their little vessel at this little town on Saturday, the first day of Sixth Month (August) 1657. This was a quarter of a century before the *Welcome* moored in the Delaware with Penn's settlers, and a score of years before the Quakers landed from the *Kent* to establish Burlington, New Jersey. New Amsterdam then consisted of a fort with a "steeple house" in it, a background of palisades from river to river which successfully kept out Indians, and a gallows prominently in the foreground, vainly designed to keep out wickedness.

The Burgher rights had just been established that year. Great Burgher-right was granted to all former and present officials, burgomasters, schepens, Dutch clergymen, and commissioned officers, inclusive of the city regiment, and to the descendants of each in the male line, provided an established residence had not been forfeited by failure to keep "fire and light," through absence from the city. From this class only could public officials be chosen. The Common or Small Burgher-right was granted to all male inhabitants who had kept fire and light within the city for one year and six weeks, and to all native born, and to those who married native born daughters of Burghers. Others, if they kept a shop, had to buy the small Burgher-right for twenty guilders. The town had already one paved street, and its thousand inhabitants, mostly Dutch, but with a percentage of several "alien" races, peacefully pursued the vocations of a colonial settlement. A copper plate view of the city made in this period is reproduced herein. This with other maps and plates appear in Volume I of Stokes' monumental *Iconography of Manhattan Island*.

The vessel looked harmless, but its cargo was destined to greatly disturb the quiet town and energetic Governor. There were eleven preachers on the ship, every one an active center of contagion. Of these, Robert Hodgson, Richard Doudney, Sarah Gibbons, Mary Weatherhead and Dorothy Waugh landed, the remainder soon going in the ship to Rhode Island, and thence spreading through New England, all to suffer imprisonment, several to endure whippings, one soon to attain martyrdom there, in the cause of religious freedom.

New Amsterdam

From Vischer's map, 1651-1654

The next day, which was the Sabbath, Robert Fowler and Robert Hodgson made a religious visit to Director-General Stuyvesant. "He was moderate," remarks Robert Fowler, "both in words and actions." On Monday Mary Weatherhead and Dorothy Waugh went into the streets and publicly exhorted the people. It is not easy for us to appreciate the scandalized feelings of the citizens. Their women scolded each other over the garden fence (or possibly their husbands over the breakfast table) but in the street they were silent.

The following shows the *Woodhouse* and its passengers as seen through Dutch eyes. It is from a letter by the two Reformed Dutch ministers, Megapolensis and Drisius, to the Classis of Amsterdam. (It may be observed that they give the date *eleven* days later than Robert Fowler does. The New Style chronology used by the Dutch was then only *ten* days later than the Old Style, still used in England until 1752, indicating an error in the date.)

"On August 12th a ship came from the sea to this place, having no flag flying from the topmast, nor from any other part of the ship. . . . They fired no salute before the fort. When the master of the ship came on shore and appeared before the Director-General, he rendered him no respect, but stood with his hat firm on his head as if a goat. . . . At last information was gained that it was a ship with Quakers on board. . . . We suppose they went to Rhode Island for that is the receptacle of all sorts of riff-raff people and is nothing else than the sewer of New England. They left behind two strong young women. As soon as the ship had departed, these began to quake and go into a frenzy, and cry out loudly in the middle of the street that men should repent, for the day of judgment was at hand. Our people not knowing what was the matter ran to and fro while one cried 'fire' and another something else. The Fiscal seized them both by the head and led them to prison." (*Ecclesiastical Records of New York*, I, 399.)

In 1658 the two Dutch ministers report to the Classis that "The raving Quakers have not settled down, but continue to disturb the people of this province by their wanderings and outcries. For although our government has issued orders against these fanatics, nevertheless they do not fail to pour forth their venom. There is but one place in New England where they are tolerated and that is Rhode Island which is the *cæca latrina* [sewer] of New England. Thence they swarm to and fro sowing their tares." (*Ecclesiastical Records*, I, 433. See also page 409 of same volume, regarding Rhode Island. "It is called by the English themselves the Latrina of New England.")

Dorothy Waugh was formerly a maidservant in Preston Patrick, Westmoreland, and later "travelled in many parts of this nation, and Jnto America, where she suffered very much by whiping & Jmprisonment, &ct, espeshally in and aboute Boston in New England, and other of English as well as Duch plantations, as may be further sene in the booke of Geo; Bishope, Caled, *New-England Judged*, printed in ye yeare 1660, to which we referr." (*The First Publishers of Truth*, 255-256.) The above account was written in 1709, and states that she had later married and lived in Yorkshire. Of Mary Weatherhead, George Fox states that she "was shott att sea by a Dutch Privateere & killed." This was in 1658. (*Cambridge Journal*, II, 336.) After eight days in separate noisome dungeons, these women were led to a boat with their hands tied behind them, and shipped to Rhode Island. The three other Quakers went to the English settlements on Long Island—Gravesend, Jamaica and Hempstead—Townships which had been established a dozen years under charters from the Dutch. Two went on, and across to Rhode Island, but Robert Hodgson called the inhabitants of Hempstead to a meeting in an orchard on the following First-day. Hempstead men were largely of the theocratic type of mind; they had their publicly paid minister, and they had heard of the Quakers. A magistrate sent the constable to arrest Hodgson, who was found pacing the orchard in quiet meditation before the appointed time. Robert says that the magistrate "kept me a prisoner in his house, but while he went to his worship many staid and heard the truth declared." This meeting, at which an imprisoned minister spoke, perhaps from a window, was the earliest Quaker meeting in this Province. The date was the

9th of 6th month (August) 1657. The magistrate, returning from church to find his house a chapel, forthwith had Hodgson removed to another house, but to little purpose. "In the latter part of the day many came to me, and those who had been my enemies, after they had heard the truth, confessed to it."

Stuyvesant, notified of the danger, sent the sheriff, the jailer and twelve musketeers (as if it were a tiger they were hunting!) to bring the prisoner and his entertainers to the city. Two hospitable women, one with a four months old child in her arms, who had entertained the stranger, were taken to New Amsterdam in a cart, to the tail of which the pinioned Hodgson was secured. Twenty miles they traveled, mostly at night. We may partly imagine his sufferings on that long tramp, stumbling behind the cart, through briars, soft sand, muddy sloughs, corduroyed bogs. Are any of us deterred by rain from going a few blocks to meeting, staying in instead, to finish the latest novel? . . . That twenty miles I covered in two hours on the bicycle, thirty-five years ago. A quarter century hence anyone taking more than a half hour to it may be warned by a busy policeman not to loiter. But then it took the night and longer. At the end of the journey the women were soon released, but Robert was led to a dungeon, "full of vermin," and "so odious, for wet and dirt, as I never saw." The prison was a small room in the Stadt Huys. This was built in 1642 as a tavern, on Dock (now Pearl)

The Stadt Huys, 1642-1690

Street, at the head of Coenties Slip. It was at this time also the city hall and court house. Robert was sentenced, without being allowed to plead, to two years work at a wheelbarrow or to pay a fine of 600 Guilders. He would do neither, so was ordered back in the dungeon, and to see no Englishmen. Brought forth in a few days to hear a paper in Dutch (which he knew not) and at which Dutch people shook their heads in disapproval, he was again put in the dungeon for a few days, then chained to a wheelbarrow, and commanded to work. Knowing he had not transgressed Dutch law (*i.e.*, a law of Holland) he refused, was beaten by "a lusty crabbed negro slave" with a tarred rope, fainted and fell, was raised, refainted at about the hundredth blow, was taken to the fort and there left all day in the hot August sunshine, where, unfed, he again fainted. Back again to the dungeon, where his mind "was staid upon the Lord." A week later, stripped to the waist, he was hung up by the hands with a weight to his feet, and beaten with rods. Two more nights and a day in the dungeon, this time without food. Again refusing to work or pay a fine, he was again suspended and beaten. A woman came, like the Good Samaritan, to dress his wounds. Her husband vainly offered a fatted ox to be allowed to remove Hodgson to his own dwelling. Citizens offered to raise money for the fine, but Robert felt not easy to accept their offer. When strength returned he willingly labored enough to pay for the coarse food he had eaten. After about five weeks he was set free, and went to Rhode Island.

It was by sufferings, in hunger, in cold, among vermin, among men cruel in their ignorance, that this meeting for the worship of God and the service of man was begun. But there must be further endurance of persecution before Quakerism was to be well established. In the meantime it spread like fire in the stubble through the untheocratic English Townships of Flushing and Oyster Bay. The inhabitants of Flushing could not accept Stuyvesant's order forbidding entertainment of a Quaker, and Edward Heart, the Town Clerk, drew up a manly protest which was signed by him, by the Schout Tobias Feake, and by twenty-eight other citizens. It stated, courteously but firmly, that they could not find it in their hearts to condemn nor to persecute Quakers, desiring "in this case not to judge least we be judged; neither to condemn least we be condemned." The liberality of the fundamenal law of the States General of Holland is noted, also their patent and charter of 1645 which they express an unwillingness to infringe.

Several of the signers afterwards became Quakers. For this manly stand in defense of their charter and their rights, Stuyvesant abolished the Town Government and set up a Dutch organization instead. Tobias Feake, who was Schout (somewhat comparable with Sheriff) and Edward Heart, the Town Clerk, were imprisoned, the former driven from the

Colony, and the latter excused on his abject apology. The Town Meeting could be destroyed, but Quakerism could not be stamped out.

Again in 1662 came persecution. Hannah Bowne of Flushing having joined the Quakers, her husband also heard the truth and embraced it. The story of this earnest pair, of John's imprisonment and banishment, of Hannah's death in London in the service of Truth, and of the charter of religious liberty attained for all by John's humble and courageous stand, is a full and vital story, rich in detail, which I have elsewhere tried to tell.* This historical background is necessary in order to fully comprehend amid what difficulties, what persecutions, at what cost of blood and tears the seed of Quakerism took root and grew in this locality.

A word now as to the Dutch colonists and as to their much maligned Director-General. What they did against the Quakers, and what they did against other non-conformists to their faith was directly caused by the Reformed Dutch Church, Classis of Amsterdam, and by its ministers there and here. Politically the Dutch felt the advisability of good relations with Puritan New England—an ever-increasing difficulty. To harbor those classed by Boston as criminals was inexpedient. But the fundamental cause of their cruelties here was the same which had driven over two hundred ministers from the Synods

---

* *John Bowne: Pioneer of Freedom*, unpublished.

of Holland, and had left the simpler church of Luther hardened into Calvinism.

Peter the Headstrong, stumping irately on his wooden leg, perverse and spiteful—the Stuyvesant we think of—is a coarse caricature of the earnest, zealous Director-General, harassed by the loss of Delaware on the south and by the encroachments of the English to the north, where they claimed to the Hudson River. While writing an important letter to tell his superiors these very things, he found time to talk to John Bowne on the eve of the latter's banishment, and, says Bowne, "he was very reasonable, and called me 'goodman Bowne.'" The popular picture of Stuyvesant is derived from a diatribe sent to Holland by a spiteful lawyer, whose description of Stuyvesant was immortalized by Irving in his *Knickerbocker's History of New York*. After the English took the province in 1664 Stuyvesant retired to his estate, where he soon died, but not before personally apologizing to John Bowne. The Fifteenth Street Meeting House and Seminary, and the Penington adjoining, are on land purchased from Stuyvesants, and once part of Peter Stuyvesant's "bouwerie."

The English, when they attained control of the province, although they levied distraints, did not persecute, nor, as a rule, show hostility. The following incident is a rare exception. William Hollyoake of Southold, Long Island, in his will, 1684 (*N. Y. Wills*, I, 129) provides that if any of his three older sons at any time "apostate from the Protestant doctrine or faith of the Church of England . . . or any of them shall at any time espouse and contract marriage with any Quaker, or the son or daughter of any Quaker, as they are now called; It is my positive Will that they shall be utterly disinherited and disowned." He entails (with this proviso) a large portion of his estate on his eldest son and his heirs forever, and leaves only a small portion to his youngest son, "who as an obstinate Apostate I reject" (and who may have joined Friends). It is evident that he is not of the pioneer type, but merely a transplanted feudalist, and probable that he had heard the charge, made in England, that the Quakers were Papists in disguise.

"First Publishers of the Truth"

There was a band of about seventy, mostly young men, zealous missionaries, largely from the north of England, who have come to be known from their travels and travails as "the First Publishers of Truth." The following were of that band.

George Rofe, coming from England in 1661 by way of Maryland, "in a small boat with only two Friends," says of New Amsterdam: "I had good service among both Dutch and English. I was in the chief city of the Dutch, and gave a good sound, but they forced me away; and so we had meetings through the islands in good service."

John Burnyeat appears to have held the first Quaker meeting in this city, in 1671, on his return from New England. He states in his *Truth Exalted*, 1691, p. 142, how he was at the Autumn Half Yearly Meeting at Oyster Bay, whence he "went to Flushing, and down to Gravesend; and when I had visited Friends there, I went to New York, and had a meeting; and then took shipping for Maryland there."

William Edmundson, a valiant Quaker missionary, says in his *Journal*, for 1672 (Dublin Edition, p. 63) "I took Passage by Sea [from Maryland] and about Ten Days after landed safe at *New-York* where no

Friends lived. *John Evans* of *Jamaica* being in my Company at that time, we lodged at a *Dutch* Woman's House, who kept an Inn, and I was moved of the Lord to get a Meeting, in that Town; for there had not been one there before; so I spoke to the Woman of the House to let us have a Meeting, who was very willing, and let us have a large Dining-room: also furnisht it with Seats, we gave Notice thereof, and had a brave large Meeting, some of the Chief Officers, Magistrates and leading Men of the Town were at it, very attentive they were, the Lord's Power being over them all. Several of them appear'd very loving after the Meeting." He evidently had not heard of Burnyeat's preaching here the year before.

This Dutch woman was the widow Matje Wessels, who for many years kept an inn by the waterside. She had seen John Bowne banished, and had kept his chest for him the night previous. She was a notable woman, and has had noted descendants. Edmundson says that she and a daughter wept when he left them. Many other earnest preachers of the word came to America, and most of these cheered the little Quaker band here, but George Fox, who came to America in 1672, did not enter this city.

The Meeting for Worship

The meeting for worship has always been the very core and center of all Quaker organization. Without this frequent gathering for Divine light and leading none of the other phases of Quaker activity would be possible. The Quaker meeting is begun with silence, and without a program. Not a mere physical stillness, but a living quiet out of which speech or prayer may develop, and surely spiritual strength and comfort, if sought. For the meeting is a means, not an end, and the mere sitting in it without spiritual effort can benefit little the individual or the meeting. Indeed, the earnest heart and thoughtful mind may find essential poise and quiet in the noise of the busiest factory or amid the myriad distractions of spring in the woodland, but it is easier for such, and necessary for many, to find it in the meeting.

> "And so I find it well to come
> For deeper rest to this still room,
> For here the habit of the soul
> Feels less the outer world's control;
> The strength of mutual purpose pleads
> More earnestly our common needs;
> And from the silence multiplied
> By these still forms on either side,

The world that time and sense have known
Falls off and leaves us God alone."
(JOHN GREENLEAF WHITTIER—"The Meeting.")

It is a practical fact, and may be experimentally proven, that regular attendance at meeting, the frequent immersion of our minds and souls—of our whole being—in the living quiet of the group, and of us all in the Divine overshadowing, strengthens our characters and enriches our souls. To quote good Quaker doctrine from a recent statement by a Jewish Rabbi,—"Creed and ceremony are but the by-paths of religion. The God realization—not the God idea—is the true essence of religion." As to the special subject of the meetings within the jurisdiction of this Monthly Meeting, the minutes show little except frequent queries as to the punctuality of gathering, and as to the clearness "from sleeping or other unbecoming behavior," therein. What we find in the minutes can never be, from the very nature of the case, more than a faint reflection through the lives of the members, of the Life in the meeting for worship. But the minutes show the concern that members should not neglect this means of growth.

James Clement, who had come from Holland with John Bowne as his indentured servant until the cost of his passage should be repaid, soon became temporarily "taken with the Ranters." A committee was sent in 1676 to learn the real cause "why he comes not to meetings." In 1682 three Friends found freedom (and so were appointed) to speak to Mary Willitts, Edmund Titus and wife and Sarah Williams, "to know their causes why they neglect coming to ye Monthly Meeting." Samuel Palmer "Declining ye Meetings" in 1687, a committee was sent to bring his answer. In 1700 a committee was sent to remind Thomas Ford "of his Slackness in attendin meetings." In 1705 the meeting "Considered the hurtfulness of Henry Franklin's neglecting meeting of Late Knowing that Such his practice is hurtful to him." A committee was appointed to endeavor to help him, but the next winter he offended by "Sitting with his hat Upon his head some part of the time of public prayer," which he later "doth condemn in himselfe or any other." Quaker men, like other men of that period, wore their hats nearly as much in their poorly heated houses as they did out of doors. They did not adopt the new fashion of doffing the hat to a superior; they removed it only during prayer. The practise of wearing the hat in meeting, and of removing it, rising and turning about during prayer, survived in certain country meetings as late as 1875.

The following "communication" to the *New York Gazette and General Advertiser* Tuesday, January 11, 1814, is of interest in this connection. "The subsequent communication having been submitted to, and approved by one of the Episcopal clergymen, we ought not to persist in withholding it from the public.

Communication:

We were much chagrined at an occurrence which took place at Trinity Church on Sunday evening during the performance of Divine service. A gentleman of the society of Friends, well known to almost every inhabitant of the city, and universally respected, from motives of piety, and by particular invitation from a member of the Church, attended service: and in conformity with the principles of his society, sat covered until the time of prayer, after which, and during the time of the voluntary on the organ he covered himself again. It is a well known fact, that all members of this respectable sect, invariably *wear their hats*, except in time of prayer: and we did hope sincerely, that there would have been enough of candor and toleration with our Episcopal brethren, to have suffered the visits of those of a different persuasion how indecorous soever their forms which they deem essential, might appear, without molestation. We are however under the necessity of adding, that this gentleman was ordered to leave the Church, on the ground of his appearance there being offensive to the congregation. It is presumed that this transaction was not known to that authority, who alone ought to have control but that it was rather an assumption of power by the sexton.

Ibid., Jan. 14th: On reading a Communication in your paper of the 11th inst respecting an occurrence in Trinity Church, I was induced to apprehend your readers might be led into a serious error as to the opinion entertained by the Society of Friends on the subject of uncovering their heads. The writer of that article appears to suppose that the FRIENDS deem it a religious duty to wear their hats during Public Worship, which is not the fact. They leave their members at liberty to uncover or cover their heads, as each one may find most conducive to his comfort. The object of this is not to justify this negative tenet of the Friends, but as the inference necessarily drawn from the article above alluded to, involves an absurdity, it is due to truth to make this statement.

A Friend."

This "well known" Quaker may have been any one of several Friends then prominent in the business and philanthropy of the city.

The earlier Quaker minutes do not always show the conclusion of any business begun. There is no clue that the committee sent to bring Samuel Palmer's answer ever came back themselves. But in 1775, the minutes being then full and complete, we learn the reasons Samuel Farrington gave for his staying away from meeting—"the want of suitable cloaths," which was not considered sufficient, "as he has been informed he would be assisted on application if necessary, and that if there is no alteration in his conduct" —he would be disowned. The Monthly Meeting afterward furnished "cloaths" and he had no longer an excuse.

I have undertaken no list of those who have preached the word among us through the years that have gone. Preaching of life and power there has been, of gifted utterance and of uncultured sincerity. Few sermons have been too short; many, alas, too long, especially for young people, who need the more a sermon than do old and settled attenders of meeting, yet can well digest only a short one. It is not that I underrate preaching. No meeting will long remain healthy where there is no spoken word. And the quality of the preaching, judging from experience, has been on the whole fairly equal to that in other religious congregations. Not even a list of preachers could be made extending beyond the memory of living members, and a mere list of names would be of little value, as the preacher does not, with Quakers, occupy the part of managing-director common to the churches. Less and less is the meeting dependent on one or more on the facing seats who are expected to speak; more and more do those in the body of the house rise to offer what of help they may to the meeting. A preacher cannot by himself make a good meeting. It is only when earnest souls unite in the common purpose and desire to be and to give, that they can become and attain. And this they may do, with or without a preacher. The naming of any appears invidious, and I will not allow myself to name any of the earnest, eloquent preachers I have heard in either branch of the Society.

Meeting Houses

The meeting house built at Oyster Bay in 1672 may be considered as a part of the history of Westbury Monthly Meeting, although the details are in our Monthly Meeting records, and their own extant records do not begin until 1697. The first meeting house built within the limits of this Monthly Meeting may be considered that at Flushing. John Bowne gave land for a burial place in the northwest corner of his plantation in 1676, "five rood long and five rood broade bounded with the hye way on the [west] and on the north." In 1692 John Bowne and John Rodman purchased on behalf of Friends an additional piece of land. In the Ninth Month (November) 1693, John Bowne and John Farrington were appointed to "take ceare to im ploy workmen to get in timber they shall see needed for ye fitting ye house for Raising against ye next 1 mo." The frame must have been raised as early as 1st Month (March) for on the 24th of 9th Month (November) 1694, Quarterly Meeting was held "at ffriends Meeting house in fflushing." This house was the easterly third of the existing house, the remainder having been added in 1716.

The earliest mention in the meeting records of the meeting in this city is under date of 12th of 8th

Month (October) 1681, when the weekly Fifth day meeting in New York having been of late neglected, and they desiring the meeting to take care of the establishment thereof, it was agreed the "ye first day meeting shall remain at Rob: Storys & ye fifth day meeting att Lewis Morris house Vntill a Publick meeting house shall be provided," and a committee was appointed to "hyer" or otherwise provide a house convenient for the purpose. The next year it was decided to purchase land for a burial place and meeting house, and to prepare timber for a house twenty feet square, but later, Friends agreed to defer building at New York, and to hire the house "yt friends did meet in." In 1683 it was thought "convenient to keepe ye house yt ye meeting was in at Yorke for an other yeare." In 1684 the New York meeting was to be at Patience Story's (widow of Robert) for the present. Patience soon after married Thomas Lloyd and removed to Philadelphia, and the meeting appears to have been thereafter held at the house of Miles Forster (or Foster). At least there is no further mention of it until 1693, when it was agreed "that the meeting at N. Yorke be removed from Miles Forster's house to the house of Rd Jones unless he give sattisfaction to ye friends appointed to speak with him." He was selling the books of George Keith, who had been formerly a Quaker preacher, but was at this time an agent for the Society for the Propagation of the Gospel (Episcopalian). In 1694 Dorcas

Jones found it inconvenient to have the meeting at her house, and another house was to be found. In 6th Month 1696 John Rodman offered ground in New York free, and a certain house of his in Flushing, to be taken down and carried to New York, at such value as the meeting should determine, but in 9th Month he and others report having purchased a piece of land on Green Street, 40 feet in front and 80 feet in length, which the Meeting accepted. The following spring a committee was appointed to receive subscriptions for paying for the land and to build the house, and a building committee appointed. Thus, forty years after the banishment of John Bowne for allowing a meeting in his house, the Quakers established their burial place and built their meeting house in this city. The deed, dated 5 August, 1696, and duly recorded in the office of the "Town Clerk" of New York, is still preserved. The lot was bounded south by land of John Rodman, west by Edward Burling and north by a vacant lot. The name of Green Street is now Liberty Place, and the stately building of the Chamber of Commerce for the State of New York covers the site of our first meeting house.

It was "without the north gate of the City," well beyond the original stockade which gave Wall Street its name. The New York Historical Society preserves a map of "the City and Environs of New York as they were in 1742, 1743 and 1744," which was drawn and presented to the Society in 1813 by David Grim,

Deed for land for first Meeting House, 1696 (text on p. 207)

Back of the 1696 deed

then in his 76th year. Number 16 on this map is the Quaker Meeting, and among the marginal outline sketches of churches and other important buildings is shown the meeting house, a steep-roofed gable end having a single center door with square fanlight, a shuttered window each side and a window in the gable over. The evident care with which the map and the sketches were drawn, and the evidences of the author's ability and exact memory, make it reasonable that the first meeting house was as he sketched it. The map published by William Bradford in 1728 shows the meeting house setting well back from Liberty Place, surrounded by the greensward of the burial ground. This meeting house was taken down in 1772.

In 1699, John Rodman, physician of Flushing and prominent Friend, who owned a plot 80 feet square on the northeast corner of Crown Street and Green Street, sold one half (40 feet) of his Crown Street frontage, running back 80 feet to the meeting house property, and also another 20 feet frontage, to separate purchasers. After several transfers both these parcels were purchased by the Meeting in 1747, and a new meeting house and school built the following year, fronting on Crown (now Liberty) Street. The *Iconography of Manhattan Island*, III, 928, states that a third meeting house was erected in 1802, 40 feet west of Liberty Place. This must have been on the same site as the second house. The map of Goerck and Mangin, City Surveyors, in 1803, shows as

Walker Street what is now Liberty Place, with an open lot (the burial ground) fronting thereon, and the meeting house setting well back from Liberty Street, and occupying the entire width of the lot. The Map of Poppleton, City Surveyor, in 1817, shows a large green area, fronting only on Liberty Street, with one large building setting back from the line. Greenleaf's *History of the Churches of New York from the beginning to 1846*, states that this third house was of brick, 60 x 40 feet, and replaced the former meeting house and school. The property was sold in 1825 to Grant Thorburn. The sites of these three meeting houses and burial ground, are all included in the Chamber of Commerce building as above noted.

Grant Thorburn, the Scotch nail maker who became an American seedsman, in his *Forty Years in America,* 1833, a gossipy account of his remarkable life, says (p. 87), "During the time I was gardening in New Jersey, I sunk twelve thousand dollars, and upwards; but when in 1825, I made the purchase of the Friends' meeting-house, this loss was *providentially* made up to me in one day, inasmuch as I paid twenty thousand five hundred dollars for the meeting-house and ground, and in a few days thereafter was offered forty thousand, and lately was offered fifty thousand and upwards. The house was situated in Liberty Street, and had been occupied by the Society as a place of burial, school, and meeting-

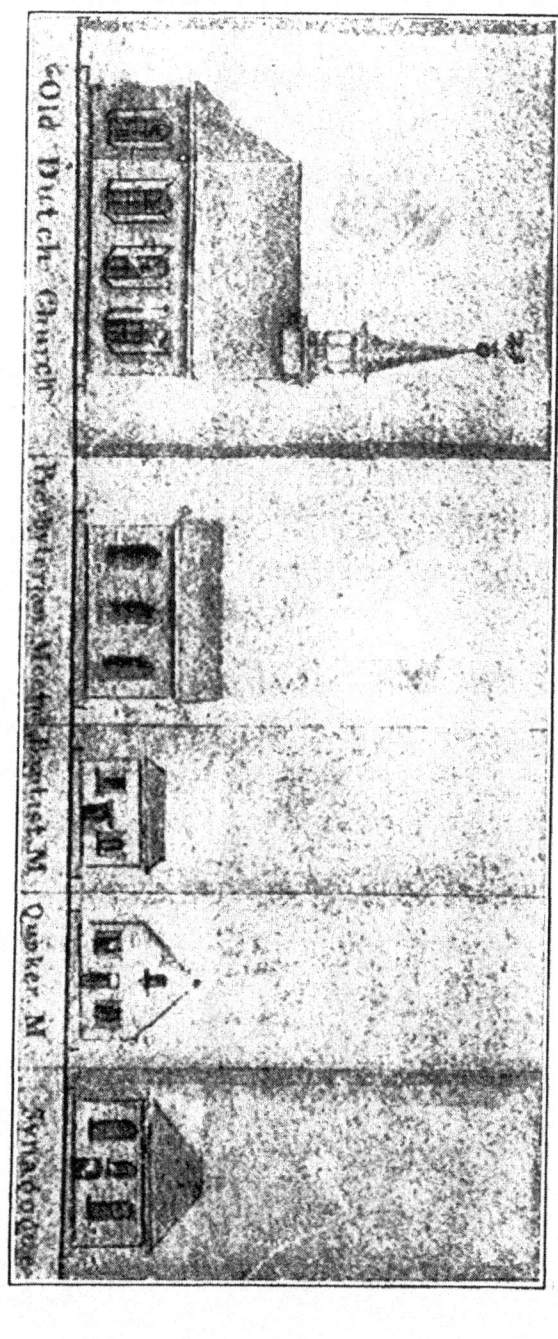

Some of the religious centers of New York, 1744
From Grimm's map

house." In a footnote he tells of making nails on the opposite side of the street. "Little thought my good friends (the Quakers) while they were paying me for nails to assist in rearing the meeting-house, that at the same time they were preparing for me a shop, wherein to sell seeds." He deems it a special providence that he was able to buy the property at a private sale, and tells of several who, expecting a public sale, were prepared to bid more (one as high as $32,000). He states that he "purchased six lots for $26,000, Mr. L. paying $5,200: so our four lots on Liberty Street, with the building, cost us only $20,800." He states that he occupied the house nearly ten years.

In 1774 land was purchased on the southeast side of Queen (now Pearl) Street near Oak Street, and opposite Hague Street. A large brick meeting house was completed in 1776. This is shown in Goodrich's *Picture of New York*, 1828, and on the maps of Poppleton and others, 1817.

John Jacob Astor, who came in his boyhood from Waldorf, Germany, beat skins in the cellar of Robert Bowne's store. He beat them so industriously that Robert gave him a silver watch. In 1786 he advertised, in the *New York Gazette*, the store where he sold pianofortes and music from London, and paid cash for all kinds of fur, "at No. 81 Queen Street, two doors from the Friends' Meeting House." Greenleaf's *History* states that this meeting house was demolished in 1824, and replaced by stores. Robert Murray bequeathed £200 to the meeting in 1786, on condition that an additional room be added within three years to accommodate the Women's Preparative, Monthly, Quarterly and Yearly Meetings, "chiefly with a view to draw and establish the Yearly Meetings in the City."

In 1819 a plot was purchased on the northeast corner of Hester and Elizabeth Streets, 100 feet on Hester Street and 125 feet on Elizabeth Street, on which was built a meeting house 68 x 60 feet and later a school building. This meeting house, built large enough for the growing Yearly Meeting, may be considered the successor of the Liberty Street house as the center of Quakerism in the city. The building was used, without serious alteration, by the Consolidated Gas Company, until torn down in 1928.

In 1819 a frame meeting house, 25 x 35 feet, was built in Manhattanville, but does not appear to have been used much later than 1825.

In 1823 land was purchased from the Reformed Dutch Church on the north side of Rose Street, 73 feet 3 inches frontage, and a brick meeting house, 70 x 60 feet built thereon, the meeting removing thereto from the Pearl Street house. Goodrich's *Picture of New York* shows it setting back from the line of Rose (now Madison) Street, below Pearl Street. The *Iconography of Manhattan Island* states that it was demolished in 1856 owing to New Chambers

Street being opened through. This house was used for the Women's Yearly Meeting, the Men's being held at Hester Street. Carriages were kept in readiness for the messengers who carried the "business" from one meeting to the other, and probably clipped along over the cobble pavement faster than the conventional "Quarterly Meeting trot." But there were no speed laws then. The meeting houses were far enough to the north to escape the $20,000,000 fire of 1835.

After the Separation of 1828 the Orthodox Friends built a meeting house on Henry Street, between Catharine and Market Streets, which they sold in 1840 to the Synagogue Anshi Chesed, having built in 1839 a large brick house on Orchard Street, near Walker. From this they removed in 1859 to the chapel of Rutgers Female Institute for a few months, and then to the present location, 144 East Twentieth Street. This last house was built by the brothers Joseph and James Hilyard, members of that meeting.

The liberal branch (called by the others "Hicksite") retained possession of the Hester Street house and school, and removed therefrom in 1861 to the present meeting house and Seminary, Fifteenth to Sixteenth Streets on Rutherford Place. The Seminary was radically altered in 1924, but the exterior appearance of the buildings has remained practically unchanged, and the tin roof of the meeting house served for sixty-five years.

These buildings were erected, and probably designed, by Charles T. Bunting (1804-1881) a member of the meeting. He had long been a builder, and at the time of the death of Elias Hicks (1748-1830) he had in his employ an Italian ornamental plasterer who was somewhat gifted as a sculptor, as his intaglio relief portrait of his employer bears good witness. This young man felt so strongly the urge to make a bust of Elias Hicks that he made the grim determination to make a death mask. It was reported in the news (*Niles' Register*) that he had secretly opened the grave for that purpose. Circumstances led to discovery and a confession to his employer, who confiscated the mask. It is now in Friends' Historical Library at Swarthmore, Pa. Much later, without the aid of the mask, or any good portrait, and without proper training, he made a bust, which was necessarily a poor one.

In 1862 the Fifteenth Street Yearly Meeting had compiled and printed a statement of what the members and meetings thereof (outside of New York City) had contributed "during this century" towards adequate accommodations for its sessions. For the third meeting house, "on Crown or Liberty Street" 1802, which cost £2,600: 0: 0, the contribution was £1,412: 2: 0. For the Rose Street house, in 1823, $5,000. In 1824 the Monthly Meeting applied to the Meeting for Sufferings for liberty to sell the property on Liberty Street, to liquidate a debt of

$22,000. This was granted, in view of the extensive accommodations at Hester Street. In 1860 the Yearly Meeting raised $10,000 to aid New York Monthly Meeting to provide better accommodations.

In 1832 a brick meeting house 40 x 60 feet was built in Downing Street, near Bleecker by the Liberal branch. This was sold and a meeting house built on the north side of West Twenty-seventh Street, east of Sixth Avenue, in 1856. In 1881, this was sold and the Friends of this meeting joined those at Fifteenth Street. The line of succession of Twenty-seventh Street meeting was from Liberty Street to Pearl Street, thence to Rose Street, thence to Downing Street, thence to Twenty-seventh Street.

A meeting house was built at Newtown in 1722, meetings having been held there from 1682 or earlier, in private houses. This was sold, and a second meeting house, more convenient for the members, was built in 1760, on the corner of Fresh Pond Road (now Clermont Avenue) and Maspeth Avenue, in what is now Maspeth, Queens County (then known as the Kills) and meetings were occasionally held here as late as 1840. The Newtown house, afterward used for a dwelling, was burned in 1844. The Maspeth house was struck by lightning and burned at an unascertained date.

The first meeting house in Brooklyn was built in 1836 at the corner of Henry and Clark Streets, by the branch of the Society now at Fifteenth Street.

This property was sold, probably because of the widening of Henry Street, and the present property on Schermerhorn Street, between Boerum Place and Smith Street, was purchased in 1857. The existing house was then built, the present school house being added in 1902.

A meeting house was built in 1868, on the corner of Washington and Lafayette Avenues, in Brooklyn, by the Twentieth Street Friends, and is still in use, though considerably altered in appearance.

At Jamaica, which was the County Town, and theocratic in sentiment, there were a number of Quakers very early, who suffered distraints for not supporting the Town's minister. William Penn was at a meeting there in 1700. In 1707 John Rodman and Hugh Cowperthwait purchased a plot 80 x 50 feet for a meeting house, and gave a deed of trust therefor. Seven and one half acres were purchased in 1709, of which two acres were soon sold. The use made of so large a parcel does not appear. In 11th Month, 1740, a committee of the Monthly Meeting was appointed to sell the remains of the house at Jamaica "that did belong to Friends." The last of the land was sold in 1797.

Concerns of the Meeting

Under the various headings following are grouped the reactions of the meeting and of the members to the "weightier matters of the law," as the Society at the time considered them, and as are reflected in the minutes. To us of the twentieth century some of these matters appear less important—some indeed to be but "mint, anise and cumin"; others, as Peace, never so needed as to-day. In the consideration of all of them the reader's mind must act somewhat as did formerly the eye in using the obsolete camera lucida, reading the fact as here reflected while seeing behind and through the fact the background of earlier conditions.

Several of the "concerns" here noted do not appear in the minutes, but were carried on by progressive minds, although disapproved by the "weighty" judgment of the high seats. For example, even so late as the 1860s it was considered improper, and so stated from the facing seats, that a member should announce at the close of Monthly Meeting (but before the "breaking" of the meeting) a gathering to establish a First-day School. This bald statement appears to need explanation. First-day Schools were then a new thing; they had not been known to the dear Friends who sat in the "gallery," and who had quite forgotten (or did not know) that Philadelphia Quakers had formerly taken an active part in the "Society for the Institution and Support of First-day Schools." That project had later become an educational rather than religious institution. The First-day School was established and maintained here for a score of years before a word appeared in the minutes about it. If it could be so regarding so unquestionably religious a matter, it is not difficult to see how it would be in matters of philanthropy not so obviously religious. Any offering of speech or prayer in the meeting for worship by one under middle life might, and sometimes did, bring such kindly advice as to "try the fleece both wet and dry," this reference to Judges, VI, 37-40, being used to emphasize the need of inspiration, of being sure that what one offered was useful; but the practical result was that only elderly, or at least middle-aged men and women spoke in the meeting for worship. This feeling carried over into the business meeting, the judgment of those on the high seats being felt to be of greater weight than that of those in the body of the meeting—felt so not alone by the weighty ones themselves but by the larger part of the meeting. The reformers, therefore, always few in number, were radicals—disturbers of the peace of Zion—and any proposition by them was likely to be calmly disapproved or ignored. Has it not always been so? And has not the result always been much the same?

Progress, under discouragement, by the few forward-looking, pioneer spirits, made lonely and difficult by the backward-looking majority. But progress nevertheless succeeds and continues wherever the pioneer spirit lives, and in very truth "the thoughts of men are widen'd with the process of the suns."

Philanthropy and Charity

Philanthropy is of the very essence of Quakerism, but its subjects have changed with the years. As to fellow members, if in want, the meeting has always looked after their welfare. The Poor Fund, for this purpose, was established early. To this day the Relief Committee annually reports that it "has attended to its duties," and only the members of that committee and the recipient know of aid given. When John Adams, in 1684, was embarrassed for money to complete the payment for a slave which he had bought, the meeting rallied to his assistance. It is a far cry from that situation to the "underground railroad," but that is considered in connection with "Negroes and Slavery." Joseph West, of New York, in his will, 1691 (*N. Y. Wills,* I, 186) after bequeathing to relatives in England, gives "to the Poor people of Boston the £50 that I lent the country for the expedition to Canada, if it bee Payed," and a residue of his estate "to be put into the hands of some honest, trusty, able men, of the People called Quakers, to be disposed of among the poor of the several churches of that denomination in London." He makes his loving friend, Miles Foster, executor, and leaves his negro girl to Rebecca Foster, probably the wife of Miles. Hugh Cowperthwait, a well-to-do but childless Friend of Flushing, in his will, 1730 (*N. Y. Wills*, XI, 107) bequeathed to Joseph Rodman, Thomas Farrington and Samuel Bowne, £100 in trust, "for ye use of ye Poor amongst Friends (commonly called Quakers) in ye Province of New York."

Now as to assisting non-members. In 1688 Jacob Telner and John Delavall of New York were appointed "to relieve a Scotch man formerly doctor robinson's servant as they after due enquiry made shal see of absolute necessity." During and after the cholera epidemic of 1798 there was great destitution in New York City which this Monthly Meeting raised money to relieve. But most of the work and expense of philanthropy and charity instituted or carried on by New York Quakers have been supplied by the members individually or in groups, rather than by the meeting. Such was the origin of the Female Association and the Public School Society, elsewhere described.

The Women's Aid Society, a charitable organization of Quaker membership, was established in 1797, to afford "relief to destitute widows with small children." It was incorporated in 1802. We have the record of cases from 1799 to 1804, which gives the names of those assisted (no Quaker names among them) and shows wherewith they were helped, in "Flour, Cloathing, Candles, Soap, Tea, Coffee, Wood, Molasses, Sugar, Meat, Butter, Bread, Wine,

Potatoes, Cash." There are several hundred entries of recipients, two of which are noted as "Black" and one as "Unworthy."

"The Society for the Prevention of Pauperism in New York" was established in 1817. At the first annual meeting, in 1818, John Murray, Jr., was elected vice president and John Griscom, secretary. Samuel Wood and Thomas Eddy were members. The name of the society was changed, together with a concentration of its aims in 1824, to "The Society for the Reformation of Juvenile Delinquents, in the City of New York." In the list of subscribers to the fund for the House of Refuge thus founded, I have identified the following New York Quakers as life members:

  Israel Corse   Catharine Murray
  Abraham Bell   Jeremiah Thompson
  Isaac Collins   Francis Thompson
  Wager Hull   William Wright
  Samuel Leggett   Lindley Murray
     William F. Mott

Among the annual members that year were John Clapp, Dr. Thomas Cock, Mahlon Day, Thomas Eddy, Jr., Robert I. Murray, Dr. Valentine Mott, Richard Mott, Robert F. Mott, Walter Underhill, William Wright, Charles Wright, all Quakers. John Griscom was a vice president from 1824 to 1833 inclusive. Walter Underhill was a vice president from

1857 to 1866. Among the Managers I recognize the following members of the Monthly Meeting:

Isaac Collins	1824-1829
Thomas Eddy	1824-1827
Samuel Wood	1826-1831
Benjamin S. Collins	1834-1844
Robert I. Murray	1837-1841
Mahlon Day	1839-1842
Thomas Eddy (Jr.)	1840-1842 / 1845-1854
Joshua S. Underhill	1844-1857
Walter Underhill	1845-1866
James W. Underhill	1847-1866

The Prison Association of New York was established in December, 1844. Among the Quakers who were members at the beginning were Isaac T. Hopper, his son John Hopper, Willet Hicks, Isaac Birdsall of Sing Sing (a member of Chappaqua M. M.) and James Brown (a member of Amawalk M. M.). The late John William Hutchinson was for years an active member.

At the first meeting of the Association Isaac T. Hopper proposed the propriety of a Female Department, which was established in 1845 as the Female Branch of the Prison Association. The name was changed in 1853 to "The Women's Prison Association of New York." The name of their "Home" was changed in 1858 to the "Isaac T. Hopper Home."

Abby Hopper Gibbons, daughter of Isaac T. Hopper, appears to be the only Quaker on the first executive committee, but the fourth Report shows the names of Mrs. James S. Gibbons, Mrs. Mahlon Day, Mrs. William Wood, and Miss Mary S. Underhill, all members of the executive committee, and Sarah H. Wood as matron of the Isaac T. Hopper Home. In 1875 there were still four Quakeresses on the committee, Mrs. James S. Gibbons, Mrs. Wilson M. Powell, Miss Ella Bunting and Mrs. Caroline V. Sanborn. In 1905 there were but two, Mrs. Rachel Powell and Mrs. Wilson Powell, Jr. By 1918 the only representative of our Society remaining was Mrs. Wilson M. Powell.

These two Associations have done a beneficent work through the years. The Prison Association has mostly worked in a public way, by investigating and reporting evils of prison administration, and laboring to secure legal remedy therefor. The Women's Prison Association has largely concentrated its energies on the Isaac T. Hopper Home, established by legacies of Isaac T. Hopper and others, and providing shelter and work for women. For some years only discharged prisoners could be cared for. Since the advent of other philanthropies, and especially since prohibition, they have been able to help a larger class of women and girls who need their help. Besides Isaac T. Hopper, his daughter Abby Hopper Gibbons and her daughter Sarah H. Emerson, were actively interested, and a daughter of the last named is still a member of the Board.

The Friends' Employment Society, our oldest extant Quaker philanthropy, was established in 1862, and has paid to deserving women more than $60,000, not as doles, but for sewing. The first women employed were wives and widows of Union soldiers then in service in the Civil War, and the first articles produced were "Housewives" (little packets of thread, needles, etc.) which were sent to soldiers in the hospitals. This led to other hospital service, and for many years the large hospitals in this city have furnished simple garments already cut out; these are given out in "portions" to the women, who are paid quite sufficiently on returning them; they are then returned to the hospitals without charge, and used therein for charity patients. The Society depends on voluntary contributions, but has an endowment fund of over $13,000.

Equally worthy though shorter lived was The Sewing Society, established in 1833 by Twentieth Street Friends, to provide clothing for the destitute, after the cholera scourge of the previous year. Twenty members met weekly at the home of a member, sewing in the afternoon, but in the evening (when incidental callers might appear) one read while the rest knitted. Their tea was a simple one, fifty cents fine being the penalty for serving cake or preserves. For at least twenty years they so wrought. Thus, in a forgotten simplicity, with little money but large hearts, they helped others and had a good time doing it. Compare this ideal with the Charity Ball type of philanthropy!

The Young Friends' Aid Association was organized in 1873. Certain young Friends of Twenty-seventh Street meeting and First-day School had felt the need of philanthropic work, but had not settled on anything definite, when Walter Shupe, a new member of that meeting, invited them to a day at his Rockland County place. There was much discussion of needs, and of ways of helping the deserving poor, and he proposed giving land for a home in which destitute children might enjoy a summer outing. This did not appear practicable, but out of that day's earnest thinking rose the "Aid," which was soon organized, and has since that time disbursed for the relief of 2,600 cases (only one of which was a Quaker) more than $78,000, in addition to a considerable amount of clothing, and with an "overhead" cost of only two per cent, this being not for salaries or rent, but largely for the expense of the annual Fair, which has long been a social event, and is a main source of income. The other principal source is from voluntary contributions. It has an invested trust fund of $14,000. The members were at first all Quakers, but others were soon attracted to join in the work and have often served as officers. The aim has always been to avoid pauperization and to help the recipients to retain and maintain their economic and social status and their self-respect. In many cases money used for relief has been refunded, with gratitude for the assistance.

The Friendly Hand is a somewhat similar organization of members of Brooklyn meeting. It was organized in 1889, originating from a concern of P. Francina Maine, daughter of James C. Hallock, elsewhere mentioned. The membership is not confined to Quakers, but most of the members belong to our Society. Its funds are obtained from small annual dues and some donations. The only "overhead" expense is for stationary and other trifling costs.

The centenary of the first Norwegian immigration brought out the fact, not shown in Quaker records, that when the ship *Restaurationen* reached this city in 1825 with over fifty poor immigrants, led by Lars Larson, a Quaker, the Friendly homes gave them shelter, and money was raised ($6.00 for each) to pay their canal fare to Orleans County, N. Y. The kindnesses of the New York Quakers is a tradition among the worthy descendants of those immigrants, and Lars Larson, who took his certificate to Rochester Monthly Meeting, named a daughter after Lydia Glazier, of the New York Meeting.

The Travelers Aid Society whose beneficent work is now universally recognized, was organized in 1905 to correlate and make more efficient the work theretofore carried on in a smaller way among many organizations. The beginning appears, as stated in the Annual Report for 1918, to have been in 1885, when the first worker was employed by William B. Collins and Edward H. Prior, members of Twentieth Street Meeting. William had brought his certificate from Poughkeepsie shortly before, and Edward's had come from Westbury sixty years earlier; they were well-to-do, and they felt the need (which is something more and other than merely seeing it).

The Society for the Prevention of Cruelty to Children was incorporated in 1875. Robert J. Wilkin, Judge of the Children's Court of this city, gives the following information:

"In 1874 a social worker visiting a poor woman dying of consumption on the west side of New York learned of a child who was abused by a woman who had the care of her. She went to several places—the police, the courts and religious bodies for the relief of the child and failed to get it because there was no law to provide for such a case. She finally went to Henry Bergh, President of the Society for the Prevention of Cruelty to Animals, and he took the matter up with the counsel of the Society, Elbridge T. Gerry. They called a meeting, at which John D. Wright, a well known Quaker in New York City, together with, I think, two other Quakers and other gentlemen, and they organized the first Society for the Prevention of Cruelty to Children in the world. I was rather closely associated with John D. Wright when he was president of the Society in New York and this story was told by him to me. I would say that Mr. Wright at the time he told me this story was a gentleman over 80 years old and I am quite sure he believed that he stated what actually happened to him. He said that one night he was awakened from his sleep by a messenger who told him that he came from the Lord and called on him saying: 'John, thee is a well-known man and the Lord wishes thee to work for the protection of children.' As a result of that message he entered the work and became the President of the Society."

The child referred to was the famous "Mary Ellen," whose case had to be considered as "cruelty to an animal," for cruelty to one's own child was still legal, while cruelty to one's own beast was not. The list of Directors shows the following Quaker names: Jonathan Thorne, 1875 till his death 9 years later; Benjamin D. Hicks (who returned to Westbury Monthly Meeting in 1865) 1876 till his death 30 years later; Wilson M. Powell, 1876 till his death 40 years later; Samuel Willets, 1876 till his death 7 years later; Samuel Thorne, 1894 till his death 22 years later; J. Dunbar Wright, 1904 till his death 14 years later. John D. Wright was President 1875 till his death in 1879.

In Prison reform, Temperance, Equal rights, and other social betterments, the Quakers of this city have been active. The New York Infirmary for Women and Children traces its origin as follows: "In 1853 in a poor quarter on the East side, near Tompkins Square, Doctors Elizabeth and Emily

Blackwell, with the aid of some Quaker and other friends, started a much needed work for friendly service to the sick poor."

What has been done for the Negro since his freedom is partly told under "Negroes and Slavery."

The Adult School and Golden Rule Club at Twentieth Street is a live philanthropy, meeting First-day at 8 A.M., and Second-day at 7.30 P.M. Coffee and rolls are served first, followed by a Gospel lesson and discussion. Thirty-four nationalities are represented in an attendance on First-day of from two hundred to three hundred men, who are in most cases not reached by any other religious influence.

The Quakers of this city—of the four meetings in Manhattan and Brooklyn—have taken part from the beginning, earnestly and substantially, in the American Friends' Service, which was established in 1917, representing the five different branches of the Society of Friends in America. The work carried on by this organization through its Committee, in relief work, reconstruction and child feeding throughout war-torn Europe has been of great benefit to those assisted. It has on the other hand been of incalculable value to the Society of Friends. Joining in a common philanthropy, represented on the one committee, the young people of all branches working together in Europe and returning home with a new sense of life and unity, the differing branches differ less and are brought nearer together. It is indeed through this work, the need for which will not cease, that the severed Society may be again united—not through any attempt to find a statement of faith acceptable to all—through Love, not Law. The story of the American Friends' Service is one of heroism, devotion and sacrifice—in some cases of life itself—which should be more fully told than it can be in this place. One result is that the eyes of the world are upon Quakers as never before, with an accompanying degree of deep responsibility to live up to the reputation which Quakerism has to-day.

Negroes and Slavery

Philanthropy in behalf of Negroes merits a separate chapter. Its development may be briefly told; how the Quaker attitude regarding slavery developed during a century and three-quarters, from slaveholding as a matter of course, like horse owning, to the "underground railroad" which helped a negro north toward free Canada with no questions asked of him, and few answered to his pursuers.

George Fox, when in Barbados in 1671, saw slavery in practise. His reaction to it is shown in what he told the masters. "Let me tell you it will doubtless be very acceptable to the Lord, if so be that masters of families here would deal so with their servants, the negroes and blacks whom they have bought with their money, to let them go free after they have served more or less, and when they go and are made free, let them not go away empty handed." As in some other matters, however, it took his followers a long time to raise their ideals to the plane of his clear insight. The system of indentured service was much in use, whereby moneyless men and women could reach America by bonding to serve for a term of years the person advancing their passage money. So had come James Clement, as elsewhere stated. So probably had come the nameless one thus described: "Run away from Thomas Rodman [son of Dr. John Rodman of Flushing] . . . an Irish Servant Woman, about 24 Years of age, of a middle Stature, pretty much Pock freckled, has a sear on one of her Cheeks, speaks pretty good English, but has something of the Irish-Brogue, she took with her an Orange coloured Gown and Petticoat home spun Made, a speckled Calico Gown lined with White, and a blew quilted Petticoat." Twenty shillings reward was offered. (*New York Gazette*, June 25, 1733.) This was somewhat akin to slavery during the period of the bond. So also was the status of an apprentice during the term of his indenture.

Job Wright (1636-1706) who was one of the trustees of the Matinecock Meeting house property in 1725, had, in 1677, bought an Indian lad. This rare case of Indian slavery was doubtless a result of the wars in New England, and the lad a captive of war. (*Oyster Bay Town Records*, V, 692.)

In 1684 the minutes state "The necessity of John Adams being laid before this meeting for their Consideration, Advice and Assistance, for some speedy supply for part payment for a Negro man that he lately bought," and a committee was appointed to procure a sufficient sum for the purpose, to be reimbursed by the meeting. In 1717 the Quarterly Meeting minutes state that "the matter proposed by Horsman Mullenix Concerning bying Negroes for slaves, them and their posterytey all soe John ffarmer proposes a paper a bout negroes the Consideration of ye matter Relating to both is Refered to ye Yearly meeting." At the Yearly Meeting the matter was "tenderly spoken two" and was referred to the next Yearly Meeting. At the Yearly Meeting of 1718, "Several ffriends declared that they were fully sattisfied in their Consciences yt ye said practice wass not Rite." In the epistle sent that year to London Yearly Meeting, it is stated that "the matter or question wheather friends might bey sell & keep negroes Slaves for term of Life according to the maner custom & practise of these Cuntries Although this matter greatly toucheth peoples intrust & maner of living in this part of the world yett a contiencious Scruple rests upon ye spirits of several friends who are willing to submit to the will of god therein as the Lord our god shall be further to make known his will and mind therein there being nothing so near to us in this world but that we hoop wee shall thorow ye help of our most gratious Lord submit it for his truth and holy name sake which matter altho of great consern was mannaged in great tenderness & consideration and is refered to the next Yearly Meeting." In 1719 the matter was again deferred; and at Yearly Meeting in 1720 was read the answer from the Meeting for Sufferings (which may be considered the executive committee of London Yearly Meeting) to our epistle about slaves, "which the meeting hath unity with" and orders it to be recorded. It does not however appear in the "Book of Records" nor elsewhere. The Yearly Meeting minutes from 1721 to 1745 inclusive, are missing, and we cannot know what became of this noble concern. I have gone beyond the limits of New York Monthly Meeting in this matter in order to show the general trend of Quaker thought in this province. In this city the convenience and profit of slaveholding was so great that Friends did not feel able to abandon it. Slaveholding was probably more common in the city, particularly in house service. In the country, slaves were perhaps less adaptable in the diversified work of the farm. At any rate it appears to be country Friends who first were active in the matter. In the Town of Oyster Bay, Long Island, Quakers manumitted slaves early. Alice Crabb having bequeathed to her daughter, Mary Andrews, "Tom ye Negro" for a term of years, after which he was to be free, Mary manumitted him in 1685 (*Oyster Bay Town Records*, II, 335) and the Town granted him land in 1697. Mary Wright, widow of John, signed an agreement, about 1700, with "her man Dick," whereby he had his freedom, but relinquished certain "Goods, Chattles Land or what Else" which might have been given him by his master. (*O. B. Town Records*, II, 453.) Yet in 1731 the estate of Dr. John Rodman of Flushing, included eleven Negro servants.

Nothing more relative to slavery appears in the

Monthly, Quarterly or Yearly Meeting minutes, which are extant, down to 1760. The cause of the matter coming up at that date was undoubtedly the visit of John Woolman. He traveled among Friends here that year, and his meek presentation of the Truth relative to slavery produced so powerful an effort in their hearts that within three decades every slaveholding Friend in the province had freed them or had been disowned for holding them. Many had made some provision for the future welfare of their former servants. Samuel Underhill in 1760 acknowledged having some time past been concerned in importing negroes from Africa, and was "Sorry I ever had any Concern in that Trade." In 1767 "A few lines was read in this Meeting from Thomas Burling, son of James Burling deceased, acknowledging he had taken a Negro boy in the West Indies for a bad debt and therein did condemn the practice of trading in negroes and was sorry for the breach of unity made thereby which this Meeting accepts." Among those dealt with for selling their Negroes (buying them had long ceased) was Joseph Lawrence, disowned in 1773 for having "sold a Negro Woman or had her sold by his order." While under dealings for this he promised to try to get her back, but failed to do so. In 1774 another Thomas Burling, who had joined meeting that year, "had exchanged one Negroe for another, that the latter he left in the West Indies where the Negroe he parted with was unwilling to go on Acco't of his having a Wife in New York." He was disowned.

The concern to care humanely for the slaves was of long standing, but being a commonplace did not get into the records. A New Jersey meeting in 1763 dealt with a member who "hath not fed or cloathed his negro in a proper manner."

The holding of fellow men in bondage was becoming more and more repugnant to Friends. The Monthly Meeting appointed a committee in 1775 to visit slave owning members. The report of that committee in 5th Month, 1776, states "there are a considerable number who are possessed of them the greater part of whom seem disposed to sett them free and some few have already complied with the advice given and Executed Manumissions for that purpose and some that have Children signified that they use endeavours to instruct them in some necessary learning but Others there Are who manifested no disposition towards giving them freedom but on the contrary the most of these Endeavour to justify the practice of Holding them in bondage." The Yearly Meeting of 1777 definitely required members to manumit their slaves. The committee of this Monthly Meeting again reported, in 5th Month, 1778, giving the names of slaveholding members. Ebenezer Beaman and wife (but they had set theirs free before the date of Meeting), John Field held two, together with his brethren who were not members. Samuel

Doughty and wife had several and declined to free them. James Way had several, and John Way had one, and neither of them would free their slaves. Daniel Latham had three, one of whom he set free but not the others. The committee in James Way's case reported a paper from him in 1779, freeing three of his negroes. A new committee was to request him to free the whole of his negroes, agreeable to the direction of the Yearly Meeting, otherwise the Meeting must disown him—which it later did. Meantime he had devised land for the meeting house at Maspeth, but at his death the meeting was unwilling to receive it. Matthew Franklin, a yeoman (farmer) of Flushing, in his will (*N. Y. Wills*, X, 17) dated 1779 and proved 1780, directed his executors "to put at interest £150, the interest to be applied to the use of providing poor Negro Children books, and also towards paying their schooling, them that their parents did belong among the People called Quakers." I have not learned the history of this fund. In 1783 a committee was appointed to visit those members who had set slaves free, to ascertain whether "something in justice may appear due to such Negroes."

The *Assembly Journal, State of New York, 13th Session*, Jan. 22, 1790, p. 14, gives an Address of the representatives of the religious society, called Quakers, residing in the State of New York and the western parts of New England, subscribed by George Bowne, clerk of their meeting, relative to permitting of vessels to fit out in the port of New York, for the coast of Africa, for slaves, and relative to a due emancipation of slaves, which was read and referred to a committee, which reported on the 28th (p. 21) that "although the committee agree in sentiment with the petitioners regarding the slave trade, yet as the right of regulation is vested exclusively in the Congress of the United States, they are of the opinion that any interference of the Legislature will be improper."

In manumitting their slaves some Friends had failed in technical points. To remedy this the Legislature passed the following act, a year before the act which gradually freed all slaves in the state, completing it in 1827:

Chapter 27, Laws of 1798. "Whereas the people composing the society commonly called Quakers and others, did a considerable time past manumit their slaves, and in several instances not in strict conformity with the statutes in such case made and provided, whereby doubts have arisen whether the slaves so manumitted and their offspring are legally free: Therefore . . . such manumissions shall from the time thereof be valid to all intents and purposes."

The History of the New York African Free Schools, from their establishment in 1787 to the present time, 1830, by Charles C. Andrews, teacher of the male school, printed by Mahlon Day, states that the "New York Society for promoting the manumission of slaves, and protecting such of them as have been or may be liberated" was established in 1786, and incorporated in 1808. Those prominent in starting it were George Clinton, Alexander Hamilton, William Shotwell,* Lawrence Embree,* Robert Bowne,* Willet Seaman,* John Keese, John Jay, John Murray,* John Murray, Jr.,* Melancthon Smith, Matthew Clarkson, James Duane, James Cogswell. Those starred were members of New York Monthly Meeting. The incorporators in 1808 included Valentine Seaman, Robert Bowne, Charles Collins, John Murray, Jr., Thomas Eddy and William Lawrence, all Quakers. Robert Murray had bequeathed £200 in 1786, to remain at interest until a free school for negro children should be established.

The African Free School was an outgrowth of the above Society. The first board of trustees were, Melancthon Smith, James Cogswell, Thomas Burling,* John Lawrence, Nathaniel Lawrence, White Matlack,* John Bleecker, Lawrence Embree,* Willet Seaman,* Jacob Seaman,* Matthew Clarkson, John Murray, Jr.* Forty to sixty pupils were taught. The minutes of the organization, preserved by the New York Historical Society, show that this school, established in 1787, had 182 pupils in 1797. In 1809 the Lancasterian or Monitorial system was adopted, this being the second school in the United States conducted on that plan. In 1815 a new brick school house, 60 x 30 feet, was built on William Street, and their school No. 2 on Mulberry Street was opened in

1820, with funds obtained largely through the efforts of John Murray, Jr., treasurer, who died before it was completed. A worthy memorial of him by John Jay, Thomas Addis Emmett, the Irish patriot and physician, and the other trustees, fills four pages of the *History*. Quakers were prominent in the work of the School, at least down to the date of publication of the *History* in 1830. In the female school sewing was taught by Lucy Turpen and later by Mary Lincrum, both of whom had been pupils in the schools of the Female Association mentioned under "Education." These "colored schools" were taken over by the Public School Society in 1834.

The work of Isaac T. Hopper, a member of this meeting, in behalf of the slaves, and so admirably told in Lydia Maria Child's *Life of Isaac T. Hopper*, will be considered together with the retrograde attitude of the meeting in the Forties, under "Administration of Discipline." His house and certain other Quaker homes in this city were sometimes way stations on the "Underground Railroad."

A mission school for Colored Adult Women was opened in 1815. It was maintained by the Clarkson Association, a board of women, mostly Quakers or attenders of meeting. I have learned nothing further of this Association or School, which was obviously named after Thomas Clarkson (1760-1846) English abolitionist, noted for his successful efforts against the African slave trade. He worked with

Quakers against slavery, and although an Episcopalian, was author of the sympathetic and excellent *Portraiture of Quakerism*, 1806.

The New York Association for educating Colored Male Adults was established in 1816. I have learned nothing of it except what is told by one thin book of minutes used in 1816 and 1817. Its meetings were held in Friends' School Room on Pearl Street. A list of about one hundred members shows nearly all to be Quakers.

The Colored Orphan Asylum and Association for the benefit of Colored Children was founded in 1836 by Mary Murray (1815-1881) daughter of Robert I. and Elizabeth Murray, and Anna H. Shotwell, daughter of William Shotwell, of the "Twentieth Street" group. Schools for those of negro blood, both children and adults, had long since been established, but the jail and the almshouse had been the only shelter for orphans of that race whose relatives were unable to care for them. Sarah S. Murray in her interesting *In the Olden Time*, tells the story, in 1894.

"Through bitter opposition they had secured a frame building in Twelfth Street for their Colored Orphans' Home, and were looking around for suitable wards. One little girl was consigned to them under deplorable circumstances, and great was their joy of heart in securing this first orphan.

"At the Almshouse, then occupying the present site of Bellevue Hospital, were eleven colored children under ten years of age. These were subjected to cruel indignities in consequence of the bitter race prejudice. Armed with the proper authority, Miss Shotwell and Miss Murray, with Miss Hetty King, always a courageous ally, presented themselves at the gates of the Poorhouse and demanded the children. The little group was gathered for inspection. But a difficulty presented—three of these were mere infants, quite unable to walk, and no conveyance was at their disposal. The girls looked at each other in some confusion, when Miss Shotwell, the eldest of the group, exclaimed, 'I know what we'll do: I will carry one, if you will take the others.' Without a word of demur, the brave young women lifted each a black infant to her arms, and, followed by the older eight, walked through the streets of New York to the Home in 12th Street."

With this as a beginning, they occupied the house in 12th Street until 1842; then, through the work of an incendiary, the Home was badly damaged by fire, and the children were removed temporarily to a place in 50th Street, which was then far out of town. In May, 1843, through the generosity of the City in presenting the institution with lots on the west side of Fifth Avenue, between 43rd and 44th Streets, a large building to accommodate about 200 children was constructed and occupied. The avenue was unpaved and uncrossable, but Mary Murray and Miss King, with the children's aid, collected stones from a neighboring field and built a rude causeway. The following account of the Draft riots was undoubtedly written by Sarah S. Murray (half sister of Mary Murray), who was Secretary for many years.

"On the 13th of July, 1863, at 4 P.M., the children, numbering 233, were quietly seated in their schoolroom, playing in the nursery, or reclining on sick beds in the hospital, when an infuriated mob, consisting of several thousand men, women and children, armed with clubs, brickbats, etc., advanced upon the Institution. They were stimulated by their success in the destruction of the Bull's Head Hotel, and without previous notice some four or five hundred of them effected an entrance, by breaking down the front door with an axe.

"At this crisis, John Decker, chief engineer of the Fire Department, a powerful, athletic man, also made his appearance with some ten or fifteen of his men. Having had no knowledge of the design of the mob to attack this building, he had sent his principal force, with two steam engines, to an extensive fire in Broadway near Twenty-eighth Street, also the work of the mob, leaving himself only two hose and a small body of men.

"On entering the building, Decker said to his men, 'Will you stick to me?' This they promised to do, and were immediately engaged in extinguishing some ten or fifteen fires, kindled in different parts of the establishment. This was of little avail, for the mob had decreed its destruction, and had saturated the floors with inflammable substances to facilitate their infamous design; and Decker was told if he repeated this act he would be killed. His men replied: 'In that attempt you will have to pass over our dead bodies.' Again these heroic men renewed their efforts to quench the flames, which were equally unavailing, and after the work of pillage was completed, and furniture, bedding, clothing and supplies dispersed among the mob, Decker saw the fire proceeding from the roof. The straw beds in the garret had been heaped together and set fire to, as well as the desks, books, maps and chairs in the schoolroom, and, having no apparatus at hand capable of reaching the roof, he was finally obliged to consign to the flames this work of faith and love.

"In a few brief words of prayer, such prayer as is not often heard, the earnest supplication for terrified and persecuted little children, the Superintendent flung open the heavy back door which had thus far resisted attack, and giving order, the long line of terrified little ones filed out, led by Mr. Davis. In the center was the nurse, carrying two babies with a half dozen others clinging to her skirts. Humanly speaking, there was no eye to pity, no hand to save. Death seemed staring them in the face. The sight of a helplessness so absolute stirred in the hearts of the rioters a feeling akin to pity, cursing was turned to blessing. And then a hush fell over the crowd, the seething mass fell back upon itself, and a passage was opened for the children. It seemed as though a mighty hand was holding them in control. A little girl, a child of eight years, was seen to detach herself from the ranks, and passing fearlessly through the crowd, disappeared into the house, from the windows of which lurid sheets of flames were already bursting forth. No one could surmise her object, no command could restrain. In a few moments she was seen coming from the burning building again, making her way unmolested through the still silenced crowd, and bearing a burden almost beyond her small strength. It was the big Bible from which the child had heard the lesson read daily for three years. And of all the contents of the great house, this was the only thing rescued. This dear child carried the treasured volume from the Asylum to the Station house, and thence to Blackwell's Island."

The report then tells how the children were all saved and taken to a police station, where they were sheltered from the mob for three days. From the station they were taken to Blackwell's Island under an escort of police and Zouaves. During this period the managers, at the risk of their lives, carried food to the station houses, for if the mob had detected their mission it would have made short work of them. The later history of this worthy philanthropy must be condensed. It was removed in 1867 to West 143d Street, between Tenth and Eleventh Avenues. It there sheltered 325 children. In 1905 a final removal was made to Riverdale, on the Hudson River, at 261st Street,

New York City. It has remained through the decades under Quaker control and direction, although others are eligible, have always supported its work, and hold some offices.

The New York Colored Mission was established at the close of the Civil War, when the colored people, just set free, were coming to New York in large numbers. It was first opened as the African Sabbath School on the day before Christmas, 1865. It was incorporated in 1871, by Edward Tatum, William F. Mott, William R. Thurston, Robert Lindley Murray, M. W. Ostrander, William J. Tanner, William F. Mitchell and Augustus Taber, all members of Twentieth Street Meeting. It now owns five houses in Harlem, with headquarters at 8 West 131st Street. The managers are still largely Quakers. The objects are "The Religious, Moral and Social elevation of the Colored People," the machinery for which are a Sunday School, a Day Nursery, an Employment Office, a Relief Department, a Sewing School, boys' and girls' clubs and social gatherings. The directing energy is still largely, but not exclusively, Quaker.

The writer has been unable to learn more than is given under "Slavery" regarding "The New York Association of Friends, for the relief of those held in slavery, and the improvement of the free people of colour" which was established in 1835. Sarah S. Murray in *In The Olden Time* quotes from the minutes of the "Friends' Anti-Slavery Society," which she states was organized in 1838 by Mary Murray and seven others. Of this I have learned nothing further.

New York Quakers have for two generations contributed to the support of the Scofield Normal and Industrial School at Mount Pleasant, South Carolina, and the Laing Industrial School, near Aiken, that State, and latterly the Live Oak School at Baton Rouge, La. They also had charge of, and contributed to, the High Point Normal and Industrial School (for Colored youth) at High Point, South Carolina, until it was taken over by the Board of Education of that City. These are all in the heart of the "Black Belt" of the south.

Peace and War

It appears obvious that any man who has an earnest faith that his neighbor is a temple of the living God cannot bring himself to kill that neighbor: equally is it obvious that all men are his neighbors, though far afield and of alien race. Nor are they alien, indeed, for the true Quaker can say with Terence, "I count nothing human alien to me." George Fox "had put away the occasion of all wars," his followers felt "in measure redeemed out of wars," and the Society as an organization has always stood for and advocated the peaceful settlement of all disputes of individuals, groups and nations. The earliest mention of military matters in our records is in the following admirably worded address:

To ye Governor of New Yorke &c.
Whereas it was desired of ye Country y^t all who would willingly contribute towards Repairing ye ffort of New Yorke would give in their Names & Summes,—and wee whose names are underwritten not being found in that List Jtt was since desired by ye High Sheriff & Justice Lovelace, That wee would Give o^r Reason unto ye Governour why wee did not Paye, or contribute upon y^t account Jt is not Unknowne to ye Govern^r how willing & readie wee have beene to pay our Customs Country Rates &c needfull Towne charges &c How wee have behaived ourselves peace-

ably & quietly Amongst o^r Neighbors, & are readie to bee serviceable in any thing wch doth not infringe upon o^r tender Consciences;—But being Jn measure Redeemed out of warres, & strifes wee cannot for Conscience-sake bee concerned in upholding things of that Nature. as yo^u yor sellves well knowe Jt hath not beene o^r Practice Jn ould England or elsewhere since we were a people. And This Jn meeknesse wee Declare In behaulf of our Sellves, & o^r ffriends, having Love, & good will to Thee, & To All Men

    JOHN TILTON MATHEW PRIAR
    JOHN BOWNE JOHN UNDERHILL
    SAMLL SPICER JOHN RICHARDSON
    SAMLL ANDREWS JOHN ffEKE

fflushing ye 30th of
ye 10th M^o comonly
cald Decemb^r 1672
sent ye 2d of ye 11th Mo. per Wm. S

 The following, from the Minutes of the Executive Council, 14 April, 1673, shows action in this matter: "The Quakers Paper about ye ffortifications considered of That the Lawes bee Attended as to Military Matt^{rs}, & his Maties Proclamation as to the Liberty granted to Non-Conformists; other Matt^{rs} relating to them to bee suspended." (*Ex. Council Minutes*, I, 168.)

 Quakers here as elsewhere occasionally suffered distraints for refusal to appear on training days, or to perform any military service. In 1759, Benjamin Thorn was disowned, being unwilling to condemn his

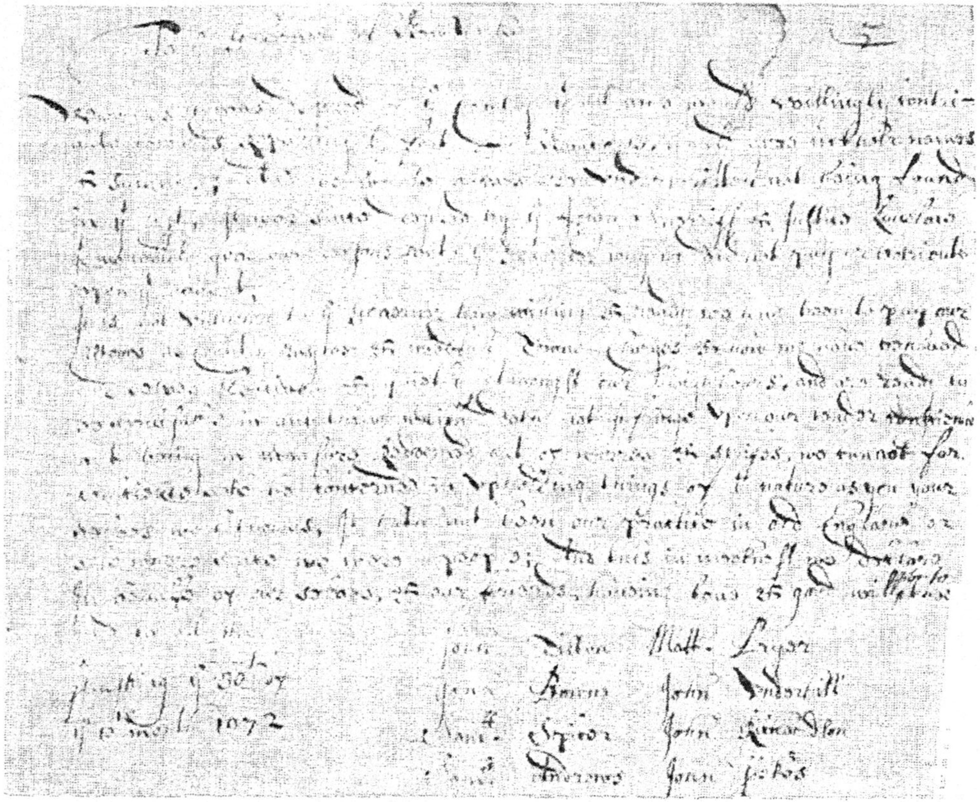

Address to the Governor, 1672

conduct in hiring a man to go to war in his son's place. By the Provincial law Quakers were not required to serve in the French and Indian war, and lists of certified members of the Society are recorded in various records. The following is from the *Documentary History of New York*, III, 623:

A list of the Names of Quakers enrolled in the office of Clerk, of and in the City of New York, in Lib: No 1 of Quakers. &c: Pursuant to an Act of Assembly, Entitled an Act, for Regulating the Militia of the Colony of New York; made & Published the 19th day of February Last, vizt:

Thomas Dobson of the City of New York	Merchant
Samuel Brown of	Do	Do
Henry Haydock of	Do	Do
James Burling of	Do	Distiller
John Laurence of	Do	Boalter
Caleb Laurence of	Do	Merchant
William Palmer of	Do	Joiner
Hugh Ryder of	Do	Shopkeeper
Walter Frankling of	Do	Do
Isaac Martin of	Do	Tallow Chandler
Thomas Frankling of	Do	Merchant
John Frankling of	Do	Shopkeeper
Thomas Frankling of	Do	Hatter
William Field of	Do	Shopkeeper
John Burling of	Do	Merchant
John Burling of	Do	Miller
Robert Murray of	Do	Shopkeeper

To the 19th of May 1755. Augt. V. Cortland Clk Co.
1756 May the 10th
Nathll Pearsall of N. Y.   Storekeeper
Thomas Pearsall of Do   Do
Samuel Frankling of Do   Do
Enrolled   pr Augt. V. Cortlandt Clk

Decr ye 1st 1756 A List of all the Money Taken from the Quakers in Queens County Persuant to two Acts of General Assembly of the Province of New York.

Town of fflushing	£	s	New Town	£	s
John Thorn	2	—	John Vanwick	2	—
James Burling	2	—	John Way	2	—
James Bowne	2	—	John Way	2	—
Benj Doughty	2	—	William Titus	2	—
Stephen Hedges	2	—	Stephen Titus	2	—
Danll Bowne	2	—	James Mott	2	—
James Persons	2	—	James Titus	2	—
Danll Lathum	2	—	Samuel Willis Jur	2	—
Samll Thorn	2	—	Francis Nash	1	—
Caleb Field	2	—	Thomas Alsop	1	—
John Thorn	1	—			

James Burling was disowned in 1759 for marrying out and being treasurer of the militia.

Benjamin Underhill, a member of Westbury Monthly Meeting, married out, "and complied with military discipline" in 1764. His case was referred to New York Monthly Meeting (which shows he was living here) and the report appears to have been satisfactory, for a removal certificate to this Monthly Meeting was issued that year.

In 1775 we begin to find references in Quaker and other records, to "the present difficulties and commotions which now prevail."

The New York Committee of Safety on September 7, 1775, "*Ordered*, That the people called Quakers, residing in the City and County of *New York*, be requested to deliver in to this Committee, without delay, a list of all the males belonging to their society, from the age of sixteen to sixty.

Ordered, That a copy of the foregoing Order be served on one or more of the most respectable of the Society of people called Quakers." (*Am. Archives*, 4th Series, III, 883.)

"A Letter from the Friends, or people usually called Quakers, was read and filed. They thereby allege that they cannot make a return to this Committee of all their males from sixteen to sixty, consistent with their religious principles.

Ordered, That the said Letter be reserved for the consideration of the Provincial Congress." (*Ibid.*, III, 896.)

The letter was as follows:

From our Meeting for Sufferings, held in NEW YORK this 14th day of the 9th month, 1775.

To the Committee appointed for Safety for the Colony of NEW YORK, during the recess of the Provincial Congress:

Respected Friends: Yesterday was laid before this meeting a request, signed by Robert Benson, Secretary to said

Committee, desiring, without delay, a list of all males amongst us, of the people called Quakers, in this City and County, from sixteen to sixty; which said request hath been solidly considered, and we are of the mind we cannot comply therewith, consistent with our religious principles; therefore hope you will not consider such refusal as the effect of an obstinate disposition, but, as it really is, a truly conscientious scruple, which we desire may at all times be exercised in such peaceable manner as to give no just cause of offence in the sight of *God* or man.

In tenderness we remain, respectfully your friends,
Signed by order and in behalf of our Meeting aforesaid:
WILLIAM RICKMAN, *Clerk.*
(*Am. Archives, 4th Series,* III, 707.)

The New York Post Boy for September 29, 1755, states that James Murray, apothecary, having received orders to send fifty pounds of old linen for bandages for wounded soldiers, appeals to the patriotism and zeal of the women in New York for aid in filling the order. In the same issue, "It is whispered about Town as if a certain Set of People [Quakers] in this and the neighboring Provinces, (and particularly One to the Westward) designed to follow the Example of their Brethren in England, in the late Rebellion, by generously giving a sufficient Number of Woollen Waistcoats to the Soldiers on our Frontiers, the better to keep their Bodies warm during the ensuing cold Season, and to enable them to perform their Duty with the greater Comfort and Satisfaction. . . .

This we presume, should it be accomplished, will largely compensate for their religious Backwardness, in not encouraging the Exercise of the Musket."

Only a few members were drawn into the Revolutionary conflict. Lancaster Burling was dealt with in 1775 for being one of a "Committee for carrying on certain Resolves entered into by the People in these times of Commotion." He was again dealt with the next year for building a ship of war. Richard Shotwell confessed that he had "thro unwatchfulness gone contrary to the Principles of Truth so far as to take up arms and assist in taking Prisoners several of the Inhabitants of New Jersey."

A proclamation by James Pattison, Major General of his Majesty's forces and Commandant of the City of New York, January 20, 1780, ordered the enrolment of every male inhabitant between the ages of seventeen and sixty. "The firemen, and People commonly called Quakers, not being within the Description of Persons hereby required to take Arms, are nevertheless expected to exert themselves in any Cases of Emergency." (*Royal Gazette*, Jan. 22, 1780.)

Among the many references to the war is one in the Monthly Meeting minutes for 5th Month, 1780, when it is reported that the Yearly Meeting had returned back £20: 2: 8 in paper currency, being such money as was "disagreeable" to that body. At the Yearly Meeting in 1779 "the new paper money"

(Continental) sent in was to be returned to the donors, the Treasurer reporting only the amount on hand "in the old money." Here we see the remarkable spectacle of the New York Friends, under British rule, sending their collection of Continental money, and the Yearly Meeting, held at Westbury, Long Island, and including Friends from upstate points held by the Continentals, declining to accept it! Robert Comly was dealt with in 1781 for cutting wood on another man's land for use in the army.

The Royal troops, probably in 1778, took possession of the large cellar of the Pearl Street meeting house, for "depositing their warlike stores." The Commissary offered to pay rent to the Friends who had the care of it. They accepted the money, but the matter caused much uneasiness and division of opinion, and was taken to the Yearly Meeting in 1779. As similar conditions would occur in Philadelphia a committee was sent to confer with that Yearly Meeting, one of the committee being Elias Hicks, whose *Journal* relates this. The net result was that the rent-money was handed back to the Commissary.

Nicholas Cresswell, an impecunious young English adventurer, was in America from 1774 to 1777, and kept a diary (published in 1924). He was verbose and bitter. Nothing in America was right. The "Yankee men, the nastiest Devils in creation." "If my countrymen are beaten by these ragamuffins I shall be much surprized." It appears quite in keeping with his snobbish nature to record, while interned in New York, "The house where I lodge is kept by a Quaker, and he and his wife are two of the greatest Jews I ever knew and two of the greatest hypocrits . . . some droll cookery here. Molasses in everything, even in salt pork."

The following document is self-explanatory, and shows something of conditions in the city and in the Society in 1782, with an old-worldly flavor of life in the little city of 23,000 inhabitants then held by the British troops, and "watched" then, as it continued to be until the police system was inaugurated, sixty years later:

We, the Subscribers, Members of the Society of People, call'd Quakers, having received the inclos'd Directions to take upon us the Charge of the City Watch, Take the Freedom of laying before the Commandant the following Representations thereon.

We acknowledge with Thankfullness, the Protection we, as a People have receiv'd from the Brittish Government, and the Indulgence we have experienc'd from the Rulers here in Matters relative to our peaceable and religious Profession; and we are desirous that Government shou'd believe that we are dispos'd to perform the Common offices of Civil Society, and bear its proportionate Burdens, so far as the same may be consistent with our Religious Principles, and the peaceable Testimony we have ever borne. We are led to believe the inclos'd Direction was not consider'd in its Nature and Tendency to affect our religious Testimony, or it wou'd not have been issued. With all due Respect to the Commandant we shall mention the ground of our objections to it. In charging our Society with the whole Duties of the City Watch, at this peculiar Time, when military works and Labour are carried on by the Rest of our fellow Citizens who at other Times share with us in Common the Business of the Watch, appears to us if accepted to be in substance "a Composition in Lieu of Military service" we cannot in Conscience support or contribute directly or indirectly to the Practice or Business of War. Our peaceable Principles also render the Business of a Watch kept altogether by ourselves, attended with Inconveniences, and perhaps so many that its End might be frustrated. Riotous and ill-dispos'd People wou'd be under small Restraint from Persons who cannot submit even to Bodily Defense, and who wou'd therefore more likely meet with Injustice and abuse themselves than be able to controul Boisterous and unruly men. The Fewness of our Number also wou'd render this undertaking greatly inadequate to the Purpose intended. The whole Number of Males who are members of our Society, and arriv'd at a suitable age do not exceed Fifty Eight. We cannot but think therefore that the Commandant must have misapprehended the Number of Males who compose the Society in this City.

We therefore confide in the Justice and Tenderness of our Rulers for that Indulgence which we only ask for Conscience sake.

We are willing and desirous when call'd to the Watch as a Civil Duty in common with our Fellow Citizens to comply with so reasonable a Requisition, and those of us who have hitherto been exempted from performing that service will cheerfully send substitutes if required.

We are with respect Thy Friends
New York 3d mo. 19th 1782.

JOHN BURLING	JOHN LAWRENCE
SAM'L BOWNE	WILLIAM COOPER
THOS. DOBSON	THOS. PEARSALL
JOSEPH DELAPLAINE	JACOB WATSON
ROBT. MURRAY	CHARLES BROOKE
HENRY HAYDOCK	JAMES PARSONS
DANIEL BOWNE	EBENEZER HAVILAND
OLIVER HULL	LINDLEY MURRAY
ISAAC UNDERHILL	

At the Monthly Meeting of 10th Month 3, 1783, Flushing Preparative Meeting reports that their meeting house "may now be taken into our Possession." The British army had occupied it, and Evacuation Day (November 25, 1783) was coming. The new meeting house on Pearl Street had also been occupied, as shown by the following advertisements in the *Royal Gazette*, Saturday, November 15, 1783.

Sales at Auction. This day, Ten o'Clock, at the Brick Meeting, a Quantity of Soldier's Cribs, Boards, &c.

Twelve o'Clock, at the Friend's Meeting, upward end of Queen-street, a quantity of Soldier's Cribs, Boards, &c.

It is perfectly natural, if war must be, that the army take public buildings necessary or useful to its purpose. It is also natural that such use damages a building. The repairs immediately made, and probably all consequent to this use (or misuse) of the two meeting houses, cost £607: 10: 0, and this expense was borne without complaint by the Monthly Meeting.

The second war with Great Britain, 1812-1815, did not affect this Monthly Meeting as it did those in the northern and western part of the State. Neither did the Civil War of 1861-1865 very greatly affect it. Several young men felt the call to preserve the Union, or to free the slaves, or both. They were dealt with, but in a more liberal spirit than formerly, and were mostly retained in membership. Illustrative of conditions is the story related in the *Life of Elizabeth L. Comstock,* p. 109, of three young soldiers learning through a chance word of the "plain" language that they were sons, respectively, of Dr. Tobey, Clerk of New England Yearly Meeting, of Sybil Jones, and of William Henry Chase, noted ministers. Of "sufferings" of New York Quakers for refusal to obey the draft law, the case of Joseph Miller of Brooklyn appears the sole one. He was imprisoned in the old fort on Governor's Island for a short time.

In the World War, 1914-1918, the consensus of opinion in the Society was that the individual's duty in the matter was the individual's private concern. That is, the Society as a body stood as outspokenly as ever for peacefully settling difficulties, but did not attempt to bind each mind to the same standard nor to fetter each soul to the same formula. This was largely due to the change of emphasis of the last half century, which is treated of more definitely under "Administration of Discipline." Out of a total membership of 1536 in both branches of the Society in this city, only twelve members entered the military service of the United States during the World War. Of these, seven volunteered, and served in the Navy, the marines, the air force, the engineers and the "greyhound" courier service. Five others, who were drafted, served in hospital, sanitation and agricultural work. Of these twelve, only three were in lethal warfare. Several members were conscientious objectors, one of whom suffered insult, ignominy and long imprisonment. What the Quakers of this City did during the World War and since, toward the work of relief and reconstruction abroad, is partly told under "Philanthropy."

Intoxicants

The daily use of intoxicating liquor was common in this country down to the Washingtonian movement of the middle of the nineteenth century. But among Friends such use of ardent spirits as produced intoxication was banned from the first, and offenders dealt with. In 1676 Abraham Whearley was "over taken with drinke" in the sight of several people. He was privately admonished "according to the order of the Gospell," and soon sent in a page-long acknowledgment, in which he expressed hope of returning to his former condition, "not in a moment, as Sum Ranters Profess to doe, but gaining it gradually as ye Lord shall give strength." A very sensible idea of conversion! A committee was to go to William Noble in 1687 to speak to him concerning his "selling of drinke," and to bring back "what he Saith," but it does not appear what he said. In 1706 "The ffriends"—later called Overseers—"appointed to speak to Such as may have misbehaved themselves" reported having spoken to Thomas Hedger about his drinking to excess "at ye Court time in Jameco." His acknowledgment was accepted, but was to be made as public as the offense.

The Yearly Meeting minutes for 1746 show that

the Quarterly Meeting had at some previous period concluded that liquor should no longer be given at funerals, but that it latterly had been so furnished in a few cases. The minutes of the Yearly Meeting are missing from 1721 to 1745, inclusive, so it is impossible to state when this ban on liquor originated.

In 1810 Thomas Eddy, heading a committee of the Humane Society, reported on "the number of tavern licenses, the manner of granting them, their effects upon the community, and other sources of vice and misery in the city." The copy of his pamphlet in the New York Public Library was one presented to "Dr. Rush from his Friend Thomas Eddy." There were upwards of 1,700 tavern licenses granted in 1809, and above 1,800 licenses to retail spirituous liquors yearly issued, while in Philadelphia there were but 190 total. The number of families in the city was estimated at 1,400, and "it will appear that one-seventh of the inhabitants are maintained by selling poison to the rest." In the retail places, "in obscure streets and often in cellars" liquor was constantly sold on the First day of the week. A great number retailed liquors "without any authority or license." The bootlegger was with us then as now, but not so much advertised.

From the daily use of spirits or wine to total abstinence the progress of the Society was sure, and was about a century ahead of the Eighteenth Amendment.

Marriage

To those unfamiliar with Quaker thought the Quaker marriage may at first appear unnatural—or indeed, too natural. But on reflection it must be seen that if the Quaker needs no mediator between his soul and God, neither do the two who have plighted their troth need any to "give away" the bride, or any to bless but the Father of all blessing. The good old church custom of publishing the banns was continued in effect by the Quakers. The two intending marriage "declared their intentions" at Monthly Meeting. Committees were appointed to ascertain if the parties were "clear of other like engagements" and in the case of a widow, to see that the children's rights were protected. If the man belonged to another Monthly Meeting he brought a certificate therefrom testifying to his "clearness." At the next Monthly Meeting, if the committees reported no obstacle, the couple were granted liberty to proceed to the accomplishment of the marriage, and a committee appointed to see if it were "orderly conducted" and to deliver the certificate to the Recorder, who returned it to the happy couple after recording its text and the names of the many witnesses. This form of marriage has stood the test of time, and needs no change. Divorce is almost unknown throughout Quakerdom.

Shakespeare said, "The course of true love never did run smooth," and he used "never" because he needed a two-syllable word right there and so made an extreme statement. But the course of Quaker love sometimes ran afield, and caused a hubbub. I use this term advisedly, for the distress of mind of conservative Friends, and the amount of space given in the minutes to "dealings" with many of those who "married out" is now seen by all Friends to have been more than the matter should have required. Yet this was given as serious attention, and as severely dealt with as certain social misdeeds which also were dealt with, all with equal harshness and with like disownment. It was considered as bad as marrying a deceased wife's sister, or re-marrying too soon, or not marrying soon enough. The phrase covers marriage to a non-member, or marrying a member without declaring it to the Meeting. These dealings resulted in cutting off from our Society many of the more progressive, pioneer spirits—a definite loss to the organization.

In the early days of Quakerism the reasons against marriage with one of "the world's people" were more valid than later. It usually involved marriage by a "hireling priest" who might be one of the fox-hunting, gaming clergymen, often in his cups, and by nature and vocation an arch enemy of Quakers, so common in England of that period, not unknown in Colonial America, but now happily met only in historical novels. A Quaker could not, in the very nature of things, so marry and remain at one with the meeting.

These disownments were mostly in the period from the middle of the eighteenth to the middle of the nineteenth century. The Society increased in members through three-quarters of this period, and lost disastrously in the last quarter. Disownment "for marrying out" may be classed as equal with the Separation in decimating the Society several times over. In the meantime marriage by a Justice of the Peace had become not only legal but popular, yet those who followed Love where it led them, and were joined in civil marriage, were dealt a like penalty with those who committed crime, and this sometimes with very brief dealings. All this is past, with other "old, unhappy, far off things," and the Discipline (of Fifteenth Street Yearly Meeting) now more sensibly advises that "marriage being a union of spiritual as well as temporal interests, presents considerations of vast importance. When the parties are united in religious faith they find not only a firmer bond of union, but greater strength and influence in fulfilling all the undertakings of life."

In 1693 Hester Smith married John "mill" Townsend, a prominent and highly respected widower of Oyster Bay. After his death she managed the mill successfully for years. But she used the Ranters' argument in defense of her marriage to one of the world's people. They (the Ranters) maintained that the Inward Light of the individual, self-interpreted, was all that was necessary, and that any testing of this by the common sense of the meeting was tyranny. She appears to have felt that God had put love into her heart and that that was all there was to it. But the meeting was not satisfied with her "charging it upon ye Lord," so after dealing with her "with bowels of Compascion & grate tenderness," they disowned her.

Daniel Deane was dealt with in 1699 for his "disorderly marriage." A few months later he "said if it ware to doe againe he would not doe it." They continued to deal with him for "going from truth for a wife." A year later he made an acknowledgment which satisfied the meeting, though what his good wife thought of it is not recorded. He "hoops to be more Care full on all occations for ye time to Come." In 1705 William Thorne of Flushing was dealt with for his "disorderly and Evil conduct in accompanying William fford and Mary Hait in their Rebellious indeavour to accomplish a marriage with out and alltogether against ye Consent of ye parents of ye Yongue woman." They were cousins of some degree, and had gone to the "priest" at New Rochelle, Westchester County, to be married. William had to ask forgiveness of the bride's father, and publish his written acknowledgment as far as the deed was known. In

1718 Susannah Slocum, formerly Hunter, "that came from the Kingdom of Ireland," produced a certificate of removal which stated her "clearness" (from marriage engagements). It was later found that the Irish meeting had not issued it, and her brother confessed that he wrote it. They were both disowned. In 1722 when Benjamin Clapp and Sarah Smith declared their intentions, "the ffriends apwointed to inquire into ye Yongue mans Clearness Returned an accompt to ye meeting that the yongue man wass intangled with an other Yongue woman So ye matter must Rest." Samuel Holmes of Rhode Island and Hannah Dickinson of Flushing, made their second appearance in relation to marriage in 1730, when Edward Stevenson objected by laying claim to said Hannah as being promised to him. The meeting could not allow the marriage, whereupon John Rodman appealed to the Quarterly Meeting on the couple's behalf. The minutes of the Quarterly Meeting are missing, but it probably affirmed the decision. Robert Field, whose daughter had placed her affections on a young man not of our Society, regrets he had not been more careful to precaution her in season, "But I confess I left her to her Liberty." In 1773 John Way, Jr., dealt with for marrying out, hoped "to be more careful for time to come." Willit Bowne, in 1778, acknowledged having "made suit to a young woman who had the privilege of setting in monthly meetings from which I Expected she would have had the privilege of being married amongst Friends, And being told by one of the Overseers she having not a Right could not pass, at which time our Engagement being too solemn to retract I went out and was married by a Priest." He was retained a member. After nearly a year of dealing, Naomi Hallett acknowledges being "too free in a light and airy way with a very loose and airy Man," but "I can say of a Truth that some gross things I was accused of the Lord knows me clear of." Of course her acknowledgment was solidly accepted. Sarah Dobson having brought a removal certificate in 1780 from Rahway, N. J., which did not contain the usual statement of clearness from marriage engagements, the women's meeting appointed a committee, which reported that they "found an engagement but she gave Satisfactory Reasons for breaking the same, & hath given the Young Man a discharge, which he hath likewise given her, which were both produced and Read in this Meeting, in which discharge he declares her Conduct & Demeaner has been Virtuous & Honorable & taken the blame to himself, the Certificate was therefore again Read and Accepted." She was married, and we may hope happily, a year later to Henry Shotwell, who probably had come from her home town. The attraction of the British uniform was too much for Sarah Pearsall, who in 1781 "left her Father's House in a very undutifull, & unbecoming manner & lived for several Days in the same House with Patrick Campbell &

was Afterwards Married to him, which Marriage was Accomplished by a Priest." This "Reproachfull Conduct," to which she was "insensible," caused her disownment. Her father acknowledged having consented to her marriage (probably after the event). It was then contrary to discipline for an engaged couple to live in the same house. It is an index of the low state of morality in the "good old days" that such a rule should be thought needful. In this case the British officer who had been billeted at the house of Thomas Pearsall, quite naturally fell in love with the beautiful and demure daughter. The merchant would as willingly have accepted a Chinese son-in-law as an army officer and a Highlander to boot. Hence a runaway match and hasty marriage, followed by forgiveness, and later the adoption of his grandson as Patrick Campbell Pearsall, the young couple having both died early.

Disownments for "marrying out" or for marriage by a Justice or Clergyman are things of long ago. And social morality has so grown that in these days (bewailed by some as degenerate and lacking in decency) it is no longer considered dangerous for an engaged couple to reside in the same house. Our form of marriage ceremony, with its sweet simplicity, is still used among us, the couple marrying each other without the help of any third person, but "in the presence of God and these witnesses," in a meeting gathered for that purpose. Variations sometimes occur; some thirty years ago as a certain happy couple passed up the aisle of Fifteenth Street meeting house to take their place, for once, at the head of the meeting, through the open windows came from the great organ in Saint George's church across the block, the full diapason of a wedding march. It was felt by all to be a happy coincidence; it was happy indeed, but it is said to have cost the groom some (well spent) time and money to make it coincide.

Music and the Drama

The early Friends—indeed, all the Colonists—were too seriously engaged in the struggle for existence to give time or thought to music. Being English they did not so keenly feel the need of it in their lives as would have felt a Mediterranean race. But as life became easier the harpsichord in the homes of the wealthy, the violin in every hamlet, contributed to the social life of many of the inhabitants. The drama was unknown in this Colony, until late. The Quakers began their organized existence with protests against the lewd songs and coarse dances of the period, as also the "play-acting," in which we may remember that no woman appeared for many years. When we consider that the old songs we love are the few worthy of survival; that the high-flavored ballads in Percy's *Reliques* represent the common taste of the period; when we note even in Shakespeare's plays, censored as they are by this editor or that, the latent coarseness which the mirror of his mind reflected; we may reasonably understand the grounds for this initial protest. It became more and more fixed into a distrust of music and the fine arts, even while the genius of the race was purifying and sweetening what had been indecent and coarse in the national literature. It remained embodied (but as a dead letter) in the discipline of the Methodist Church until 1924.

But some Friends fell away from this "testimony." Samuel Burling made acknowledgment in 1771, of attending a "Consort of Musick," and Samuel Cowperthwait acknowledged in 1773 that he had been "at a play, which has been cause of trouble to me as well as uneasiness to my friends." Well it might, for the first theater in the city, built in 1750, had not been patronized, and was made into a church for the German Calvinists in 1754. The second theater, of 1758, was torn down by a Stamp Act mob in 1764, the actors having been forewarned that amusements and expenses did not suit the solemnity and the public distress of the times. In the third theater, built in 1767 on John Street, Shakespeare's plays were produced, one of which we may suppose was the cause of "uneasiness" to Samuel's friends. In 1781 Major Andre and other British officers began producing plays, one of which was probably seen by William Titus, but besides going to the play he dealt in Prize goods (goods captured by a privateer) and had played at cards, and it is a question which was considered the greater evil. He was read out. The play seen by Samuel Cowperthwait may well have been Hamlet, which George Washington notes that he saw here in 1773.

This distrust of art, like the distrust of hospitals

by the ignorant (and about as rational) remained embodied in the Discipline until well past the middle of the nineteenth century, when the wording of the Query was changed to read "places of amusement of a hurtful tendency," and dealings against the enjoyment of music or the drama ceased. The kindergarten in Friends' Seminary had to have a piano, but at Yearly Meeting time it was placed sufficiently out of the way so that it was out of sight. This went on until about 1895, when a few of the younger ones, at the suggestion of an elderly Friend from the country, unearthed it for a social evening at the close of Yearly Meeting. It never again disappeared, and social dances in the gymnasium at Fifteenth Street have been occasionally held.

For a good many years Friends have freely patronized the better plays, and references to them are heard in sermons. The young Friends used to give little plays, light and humorous, in the library at Fifteenth Street thirty years ago. The Young Friends of to-day produce such plays as *The Servant in the House;* they give them in the meeting house, and give them withal in a spirit of worshipful service.

Administration of Discipline

The "papers of advice" of George Fox were read at stated periods in the meeting. Care was taken that the youth and servants (including slaves) should hear them. The Book of Discipline of every Yearly Meeting has been developed from these quaint but salutary advices. Philadelphia Yearly Meeting attempted a codification of the discipline in 1704, and revised this in 1719. New York Yearly Meeting minutes for 1760 show that this Philadelphia discipline had been long in use here, and a revision of it was made in the next two years. As the Yearly Meeting minutes are missing from 1721 to 1745 inclusive, we cannot know the early development of this document destined so profoundly to affect the Society. As it became more and more codified, more and more rigid, what had been an expression of the fervent humanity of Fox became a Procrustean measure of conduct. This, as has been pointed out, went along with a lessening of spirituality. The Society became free from persecution, and suffered little from distraints. Members were relieved of military service. They had become well-to-do in general, some wealthy. But the Discipline, while governing the many was known only to the few. Each Monthly

Meeting had one manuscript copy. When the first printed edition was put forth, in 1800, two copies were to be delivered to each business meeting, and the copies then in use were to be given up to the Meeting for Sufferings (Representative Committee, the executive committee of the Yearly Meeting) to be destroyed; as a result of this there are preserved but very few copies of the manuscript Discipline, which escaped the vigilance of the committee. Some of these rarities are finely engrossed on parchment. It was not until the edition of 1810 that any member might own, or readily see, except by courtesy of the Clerk, the Discipline by which he was expected to live. Under these conditions a rigid administration of the rules was maintained. Disownments were greater in number, and for more trivial offenses (as we now see the matter) in the period from the middle of the eighteenth to the middle of the nineteenth century. All this is long past, and the simplification of the Discipline, coupled with a kindlier administration of it, progressed about equally at Twentieth Street and at Fifteenth Street, until now, when the Discipline may be said to be lived rather than administered.

As a matter of history, in which the evil should be shown equally with the good, and the lesson drawn from both, the one "awful example" of the hard legality of "dealing" and abuse of power may be given. During the unfortunate century of disownments the Society lost many for offenses we now think trivial, but this was an extreme case.

Isaac T. Hopper, the noted Abolitionist, a convinced Friend (*i.e.*, not a birthright member, but received on his own request) after an active life in Philadelphia, where his vocation was bookselling and his avocation the freeing of slaves, came to this city in 1829, and maintained for several years a book store for the sale of Quaker literature. He, with his son-in-law, James S. Gibbons, and his friend Charles Marriott, all members of the Monthly Meeting, became members of "The New York Association of Friends, for the relief of those held in slavery, and the improvement of the free people of colour," which was established in 1835, and composed solely of Quakers. This organization was denied the privilege of holding its meetings in the meeting houses, "and," says Isaac T. Hopper, "one Friend, in the station of a minister, said he would as soon go to the theatre as to attend any of the meetings of our association." The attitude of the meeting had sadly changed from that of sixty years earlier. By 1841 the merchants who dealt with the South in cotton, sugar, or other produce or goods (New York was then a greater market for the South than now) and the local press, reflecting the business feeling, were pro-slavery in sentiment to a marked degree. The portion of the meeting which sat on the high seats, and did the talking in business meeting—the vocal part of the Society—frowned on the Abolitionist movement. George F. White, a minister much loved by some, was especially prejudiced against all disturbing reforms, and in his preaching stigmatized the anti-slavery workers as "hireling lecturers," "hireling book-agents" and "emissaries of Satan," and stated his position thus plainly—"I had a thousand times rather be a slave, and spend my days with slave-holders, than to dwell in companionship with abolitionists." I have heard it stated or insinuated that George F. White was interested financially in the sugar trade. I am inclined to doubt this, as the city directory shows him a flour merchant, at least from 1838 to 1842. Flour from this state and westward was then brought on the Erie Canal in large quantities for export and perhaps to some extent for the southern trade. Isaac and his friends were at this time in the executive committee of the Anti-Slavery Society. *The Anti-Slavery Standard,* the organ of that Society, published an editorial entitled, "Rare Specimen of a Quaker Preacher," which criticized such utterances, giving quotations from White's sermons. Isaac had not seen the article until it was published, but he, with Gibbons and Marriott, were dealt with by the Monthly Meeting, on a charge of "being concerned in the publication and support of a paper calculated to excite discord and disunity among Friends." They were disowned in 8th Month, 1841. Isaac appealed, and the dealings lasted half a year, being carried on appeal to the Quarterly, and thence to the Yearly Meeting of 1842, where a committee of thirty-six, after six two-hour sessions, reported eighteen for confirming the decision of the lower meetings, fifteen for reversing it, and three who declined to pass judgment. The Yearly Meeting confirmed the disownment on this narrow margin. And this in face of the custom of general consent—that unanimity universal in Quaker business meetings. I have found no other instance of a decision by numbers in a Quaker Meeting. Thus was separated from the Society one of the best men and truest Quakers who ever belonged to it. Sixty years earlier the Monthly Meeting had disowned the last member who would not free his slaves. Now, as merchants dealing in the products of other men's slaves, or allied in business with such, influenced by the pro-slavery tone of the newspapers, and *not spiritually awake,* the meeting disowns the Abolotionist. He continued to sit on the facing seat, under the ministers' "gallery" to the end of his days. Orthodox Friends were concerned that the public should not think it was their Meeting which had disowned him. His *Life* by Lydia Maria Child, is as entertaining as a fairy tale. Of his death she writes, "No public buildings were hung with crape, when news went forth that the Good Samaritan had gone. But prisoners, and poor creatures in dark and desolate corners, wept when they heard the tidings." His *Narrative of the Pro-*

ceedings of the Monthly Meeting of New York . . . in the Case of Isaac T. Hopper, 1843, from which I have made quotations, tells the sordid story in detail, from his point of view, which is borne out on the essential points by the minutes of the meetings. From that day to this many members have regretted the official action of the Monthly Meeting, and something in the nature of a reinstatement of his membership was proposed thirty years ago. Such an act would be futile. The name of Isaac T. Hopper needs no certification from the meeting, nor could such an act of penitence remove reproach from the Quaker name. Rather should we profit by it, in keeping our own minds more free from prejudice than were some in the past.

This retrograde attitude was not confined to one branch of the Society. Charles Collins (1774-1843) son of Isaac, the printer, had steadfastly borne the testimony against articles of slave manufacture. Sharing a Friend's umbrella, and noticing that it was of cotton, he insisted on walking home in the rain. Purchasing tracts at the Anti-Slavery Society, he would not allow them to be tied up with a string of southern cotton. Shortly before his death the pro-slavery attitude—or lack of an anti-slavery attitude—in his meeting (Twentieth Street) caused him to send in a resignation of his membership, but it was not read.

Willett Hicks was a portly, dignified Friend of

style and distinction, with carriage and footman. He was an eloquent minister in Twentieth Street Meeting and was called (by outsiders) the "Bishop of the Quaker Church." He was "liberated" for a religious visit to England in 1819, and on his return Friends found that he had combined his "concern" with the purchase of a large amount of goods which he sold here at a great profit. He was dealt with, but nothing came of it.

The tone of the present disciplinary "Advices" would have been useful in the past—"they who would do the Father's work must abide in His love. Even a seeming harshness may check the beginnings of true repentance, and a lack of sympathy cause harm where only good was intended."

"If Differences Arise"

The Discipline advises, that in cases such as this heading intimates, there should be "due care taken speedily to end them." Our minutes show disputes arbitrated by a committee, and "dealings" with a refractory member who would start a suit at law against a fellow member instead of using the friendly method of arbitration. A few examples will show how simple such a settlement is, but a depth of spirituality, a mellowing of the whole nature, must occur before it may be so sweetly accomplished. When Samuel Haight and Daniel Kirkpatrick had a difference in the 4th Month (June) 1700, which they could not end between them "they both have left it to friends of this meeting to make a final end of ye difference and doe promise to be fully Sattisfied with friends determination." It was left until the "faull" for "finall Issew," which undoubtedly was satisfactory, as nothing further appears about it. The next year Daniel had another difference, this time with Thomas Hedger. It was "arbytrated & a Judged" by twelve good men and true, named by the meeting with the approbation of both parties. Three months later they "Did freely voluntary & Lovingly accquit Each other, & did Mutually take one another by ye hand promising to forgett & forgive Each ye other & further that wherein they had don amiss for ye time Past, they would Endevor to Do So No more, in Testimony whereof they have heere unto set their hands." The clerk's record bears their autographs.

In 1753 Daniel Lawrence acknowledged that "my Stoping my Brother Stephen upon the highway where he was Going to Cary my hogs to pound was not warrantable." Town rules and Provincial laws authorized the impounding of hogs, or their killing if found on common land or in highways. But Daniel, in cool afterthought, hoped he should thereafter "Live like a Brother with him." Samuel Burling expressed penitence for what happened between Isaac Willits and himself, "and tho' his injurious and unmanly Conduct appeared to me highly provoking, yet I am sensible the part I acted in striking him was inconsistent with our Christian Principles." For a Friend to bring a lawsuit against a fellow member without first asking the meeting to judge the matter, would inevitably have brought "dealings" on himself, and perhaps disownment. Lawsuits against non-members were likewise allowable only on approval of the Monthly Meeting. The Discipline has not weakened in this matter.

Language

It happens that Quakers have done somewhat toward preserving the English language from impoverishment. The great majority of the first generation were from the counties and smaller towns of England, where the Saxon speech had longest survived, and where more words of Saxon origin were used than by London-bred writers.

There has been a noticeable preponderance of Saxon words over those of Latin origin in the minutes and Disciplines, and to some degree in Quaker books published, down almost to the present day, and some Saxon forms appear likely long to remain in use among Quakers. With them "Yearly Meeting begins" with others the "Annual Conference commences." They "gather," where others "congregate." Other Saxon words I have herein occasionally given in quotation marks, where their appearance in the sentence may be unfamiliar to the reader.

Of words of Latin origin they have retained some meanings which have been so generally forgotten in the changing language that we alone retain them. "Concern" is typical of these, the *Standard Dictionary* giving as one of its rarer meanings, "a feeling of obligation to perform a religious duty, used by members of the Society of Friends." And only recently have they yielded to the habit of splitting the infinitive—"speedily to end them" will be acknowledged to have a better sound than "to speedily end them." They still retain, now only as a pronoun of affection, "thee," and for this they are criticized as ungrammatical, because they use it both for nominative and objective cases. But, dear reader, in this case (or these cases) thee may recall how English has changed with the centuries, and even with the decades, so that such thoughtful critics as Brander Matthews and Professor Lounsbury have had a kind word even for the split infinitive. These scholars contend that use makes and changes language, and that the lexicographers and grammarians trail after, but far behind, with recognition of the changes. On such ground the Quakers may claim propriety for their long use of "thee" for second person, singular.

The use of the "plain" language, the care to speak exactly, to make their words as lucid as their lives, above all, to avoid overstatement—does not this help to explain the fact that a Quaker * (not college bred) compiled a Grammar of such effect on English language and literature that on the centenary of his death the *New York Times* devotes a full column editorial to his memory? Does it not help to account for a later Quaker † whose Grammar was a standard for three-quarters of a century?

* Lindley Murray.
† Goold Brown.

Moderation and Plainness

I need not quote examples from the records to illustrate this concern. The fervent honesty of thought and hatred of sham, the innate democracy with which the spirit of George Fox imbued the early Friends, was the basis of their plainness. Attention to that within us which is best inevitably leads to moderation in all things (albeit difficult for some of the active spirits of all times).

The "plain" dress of early Friends was the ordinary clothing devoid of the customary ornamentation. The average man wore the "hodden gray" which Burns immortalizes. Wealthier Quakers soon adopted the same. When new was needed it was not common sense to seek a new style. The pattern and color therefore changed only slightly, little by little, to the Quaker dress our eyes have seen. It is too well known how Plainness became a form—an end in itself—and so remained to the hurt of members and to the loss of the Society, until divine common sense reasserted itself and condemned to the discard that shell of Plainness, retaining a real simplicity of life and thought, not as an end but as a measure to real happiness. Quakers are to-day generally less given to show than the average, and, I believe, more simple and moderate in their lives. The general attitude of Quaker thought on this theme may be summed up thus: having wealth, not to exploit it; having robust health, not to live extravagantly; having power, not to exert it all; having speed, still to drive leisurely. These restraints are of the essence of gentle living, and conduce to the happiness desired by all. The principle of simplicity does not change with the years or centuries, but the manifestations of it change with the varying conditions of life. We should endeavor so to keep our lives and possessions as to avoid ostentation and display; to keep our minds free from the burden of fashions, and our souls steadfast in a changing world.

Equality of the Sexes

Quakers have been noted for their recognition of women's equality with man, but have not been altogether worthy of this reputation. Elizabeth Hooton, the first woman convinced by George Fox's preaching, and the first Quakeress to appear in the ministry, established equality as to that service. And the earliest minutes reflect the deep-seated feeling of equality of Fox. Anthony Wright, in his deed of gift for land for the meeting house at Oyster Bay in 1672, conveyed it to four trustees, three of whom were women. But it was not common, nor indeed desirable, for a woman to own property, as on marriage it automatically became the property of her husband, who henceforth could dispose of it as he thought best. The influence of old custom soon affected the Society, and a marked difference of status shows in the records as to nearly everything except preaching, which has remained equally acceptable, from both men and women. The Disciplines of both branches of the Society, until after the middle of the nineteenth century, still described in detail the organization and inter-relation of the (Men's) Meeting for Discipline (business meetings) and after that took up a brief description of "Women's Meetings." The men's Monthly Meeting received in membership, or disowned therefrom, individuals of their own sex without notification to the Women's Meeting. The women, on the other hand, informed the men's meeting of their action on all disciplinary matters, and acted only "if the men's meeting unites therewith." If the men did not unite the women's action was void. Sometimes the men sent the matter back for further consideration, occasionally appointing a committee to confer with one appointed by the women. The women's meeting at times requested the assistance of men Friends in a difficult case. Certificates for women were accepted by the women's meeting at first, but soon they reported them to the men, who also accepted them, while certificates for men were not reported to the women's meeting.

As late as 1895 the Property Committee of Fifteenth Street Monthly Meeting had no women members; the matter of their inclusion being brought up at that time, a few elderly men offered what they considered grave objections. By the end of the century a few women were appointed, and we may consider that date as the beginning of actual and complete equality in meeting affairs at Fifteenth Street. At Twentieth Street the Discipline declared in 1874 that "the rights and privileges of membership are to be in no way affected because of sex," yet no woman has yet been a member of the Property Committee. This is not owing to objection by the men, but rather that having equality in the charter it does not appear necessary to emphasize it in practise.

The majority of Friends in this city, as elsewhere, were in favor of equal suffrage long before the passage of the Nineteenth Amendment. A very few however were so sincerely opposed to the idea that no united pronouncement could be made on the subject. These few lived to see their wives and daughters at the polls, and to pronounce it good.

As elsewhere stated, in some reforms the Quakers were not quite ready; in this one especially. Although they had the reputation of equality, they had early lost and have but lately recovered, the spirit of equal opportunity and service regardless of sex.

Quakers in Civil and Public Life

One of the larger errors of American Quakers was the withdrawal from the political life of the community and the State. Although South Carolina and New Jersey had each a Quaker governor, and Rhode Island had several (one of whom served seven terms) and although the government of Pennsylvania was for three-quarters of a century entirely in Quaker hands, a general reaction set in, intensified by the Pennsylvania Quakers refusing election. The Discipline thereafter advised against, and queried after, the acceptance of "Posts of profit or honor." Latterly a few American Quakers have held political office, even in the houses of Congress and in the Presidential chair.

Quakers were sometimes shut out from public office by laws or unlawfully by officials. John Bowne was appointed Treasurer of Queens County in 1683 by the representatives from the Towns, and served. He and Thomas Pearsall were elected in 1691 as Representatives to the General Assembly, but while "willing to sign the Test, and engage to perform the Tenor of the Oaths under the Penalty of Perjury," they were not seated. (*Journal of Gen. Assembly, Lott's Ed.* 1764, I, 2.) The Assembly passed an Act at that session intended to give relief from the oath, but appears to have failed in its purpose. Miles Foster, chosen 1697 Collector for the East Ward, was declared ineligible for service by the court of Mayor and Aldermen, because he was a Quaker. (Minutes of that Court, in Stokes *Iconography*, IV, 399.)

The Colonial Assembly passed an Act in 1734, granting to the Quakers the same privileges and benefits as by the laws entitled to in the Kingdom of England, Dominion of Wales and Town of Berwick upon Tweed. Yet justices without oath had been allowed 1678. This was in regard to oaths, the simple affirmation being lawful instead, for Quakers. If not publicly known for some years before his or her affirmation, a certificate from the Quarterly Meeting, signed by six or more of the principal people, was required.

Shut out from political life even more by their own restrictions, Friends proved themselves public spirited, and competent to develop and execute their civic ideals. Perhaps it was this very abstention which led the minds and hearts of many into works of philanthropy, but I think they would have accomplished more good had they tried to show that politics may be clean. Who knows how much cleaner and more rational the local politics might have been had Quakers participated therein, as earnestly and effectively as they did in non-political reforms? The Quakers here noted were citizens of note in their day, and were, except for the few so stated, members of New York Monthly Meeting.

William Bradford (1660-1752) though never a member here, may be mentioned. He had come with Penn in the *Welcome* in 1682 and had returned the following year to marry Elizabeth Sowle, daughter of Andrew, in whose Quaker printing shop he had served his apprenticeship. He proposed to publish in 1688 the first English Bible in America, but did not receive sufficient subscriptions. He became the authorized printer for Philadelphia Yearly Meeting in 1690. The accounts of John Bowne show purchases of books and stationary from him; and an authorization to Bowne to sell books on commission, in 1688, is preserved in the N. Y. Public Library. He printed a book for George Keith, and appears to have taken up the latter's repudiation of Quakerism, for which he was disowned in 1692. Keith had been an eminent Quaker preacher, but left the Society and became prominent and active as an agent of the (Episcopalian) Society for the Propagation of the Gospel. Bradford removed to New York in 1693, where he was for thirty years the Royal printer, and only printer, in the colony. He had a country place at Oyster Bay. In 1725 he began the *New York Gazette*, the first newspaper in the Colony. His name does not appear in our records, but his wife, Elizabeth, witnessed two marriage certificates, at Matinecock, in 1698.

Isaac Collins (1746-1817) was born a member of the Society in New Jersey, and was commissioned in 1770 as Printer to the King for that Colony. He printed the Provincial currency, laws, etc., and in 1771 began printing the *New Jersey Almanack*, which he continued for twenty-six years. He reprinted Sewel's *History* and other Quaker books for the Quakers, and Baxter's *Saint's Everlasting Rest* for the Methodists. In 1791 he completed the printing of the first quarto edition of the Bible in America, five thousand copies. Besides the concern shown in Quaker records that Friends should subscribe for this, the Presbyterian General Assembly and the Baptist Association each recommended it to their constituents. The care he used is shown by the fact that while several other people read the proofs of the Bible, his own children read them eleven times, the last time at the rate of one pound sterling for every error found. The only inaccuracies found in the end are said to have been one broken letter, and a punctuation point. He removed to this city in 1799, and opened a printing office at 189 Pearl Street. He was a member of the Public School Society, and interested in other philanthropies.

Walter Bowne (1770-1846) was a hardware merchant, who became Grand Sachem of the Tammany Society in 1820, represented this city in the State Senate 1824 to 1827, and was appointed Mayor by the Common Council (which then had that power)

1827 to 1831. But he appears to have left the Society of Friends after he acquired wealth and long before he went into politics. He was later in many public affairs.

Walter Underhill (1827-   ) appears to have been the only Quaker Congressman from this city until recently. He was in the House of Representatives. He was disowned in 1854, in connection with a failure in business.

Thomas Eddy (1758-1827) was called "the Howard of America." From his biography by Colonel Samuel L. Knapp, 1834, I glean the following. His portrait, from a painting by W. Dunlap, N.A., shows a rather slender man (muscular and compact, says his chronicler) with a thin long head, plainly severe in face and severely plain in dress. His firm, Eddy, Sykes and Company, did a general commission business. The correspondence given by his biographer shows him intimately associated with three Governors of the State, George and De Witt Clinton and John Jay, also with Chancellor James Kent, with Cadwallader D. Colden, the eminent lawyer and statesman, with Robert Fulton, and others less well remembered, but all noted in their day. He was a classmate with John Murray, Jr., at Friends' Grammar School in Philadelphia about 1770, and read his memoir of Murray before the governors of the New York Hospital in 1819. Although he had received only an elementary English education, he felt that the intellectual culture of the Quakers was behind that of many other religious communities. Would that he had as successfully undertaken to remedy that as he did other evils! With General Philip Schuyler, then a State Senator, he secured the establishment of a State Prison. The commissioners were Matthew Clarkson, John Watts, Isaac Stoutenburgh, John Murray, Jr., and himself. These made him the committee to build it. His election as a governor of the New York Hospital marked the beginning of great improvements in its work and scope. It is due to him that Bloomingdale Asylum was established in 1818. He was a governor of it for twenty-eight years. He had a profound influence on the Legislature, and appeared before it frequently on behalf of these and other philanthropies. His work for and among the Indians of New York and eastern states occupies a large portion of his biography.

He helped to promote the Erie Canal, being one of the State commission in 1810 which inspected the proposed route and recommended the canal. He was one of the original directors of the Western Inland Lock Navigation Company, and continued as director and treasurer until the company disposed of their property in 1820 to the State, which thereafter continued and completed their work, resulting in the Erie Canal.

He was connected with the New York Bible Society from its organization until his death. He was an active member of the Chamber of Commerce, which now stands on the site of the meeting house where he was married. He was one of the founders of the "Society for Promoting the Manumission of Slaves" and of the "Society for the Prevention of Pauperism." In 1793 he was one of the members to receive donations for "The Society for the relief of Distressed Prisoners." This had been organized in 1784 for the benefit of those imprisoned for debt. He published the *Account of the State Prison*, elsewhere mentioned, and *Hints for introducing an improved mode of treating the insane in the Asylum*, 1815.

John Hartshorne Eddy (1783-1817), son of Thomas, was a deaf mute, but studied botany at Columbia College, 1809-1810, mastered the Linnean system, and subsequently became a practical botanist. Had his life been prolonged he might have secured a permanent place in the roster of American botanists. He was also a good cartographer, publishing in 1812 his circular map of "Thirty Miles around New York." His large map of New York State, in the engraver's hands at his death, and published in 1818, was "the best that had ever been drawn of it," says Samuel L. Knapp, and a yellowed copy of it in the New York Public Library bears out that statement.

Robert Murray (1714-1786) whose firm, Murray, Sanson & Co., was the largest shipping organization in this country, had one of the first private coaches in the city, imported from London, probably similar to that of James Beekman, preserved by the New York Historical Society. His "leathern conveniency" he called it. The itemized bill for it amounting to £153: 14: 0, may be seen in *In The Olden Time*, by Sarah H. Murray, where much of interest relating to this family, and early New York, is recorded. His country place was at Incluberg, now called Murray Hill, and the Grand Central Station occupies what was one of his cornfields. His wharf property, at Coffee House Slip and Wall Street, was the most prominent one in the City. Here public sales were conducted; here docked the principal merchant ships; here in 1774 docked Captain Chambers, with tea, and here on an April evening did "Mohawks" board his ship and dump eighteen cases of that tea overboard. Here also did Washington step ashore from a barge, to become our first President. It was Robert's wife, Mary, who so graciously entertained the British officers with cakes and wine, their troops standing at ease, the while that General Putnam was getting his little army out of reach of his pursuers. The story of this is entertainingly told in *In The Olden Time*.

John Murray (1720-1808) brother of Robert, was a wealthy merchant and was the eleventh President of the New York Chamber of Commerce, 1798 until 1806, when on being again elected he declined office. His house was in St. John's Square. The fine trees which were felled to make a railroad freight terminal out of this charming spot were planted by him.

Lindley Murray (1745-1826) son of Robert, began his education in 1752 in the Friends' School at Philadelphia, continued it under a private tutor, and studied law in the office of Benjamin Kissam, with John Jay for a fellow student. Admitted to the bar in 1765, he practised until the Revolutionary War made that unprofitable, then was a merchant in connection with his father for a few years, when he retired to his country place, Bellevue. Had the great hospital which has stood on this site since 1816, and bears this name, been then in being, his subsequent story might have been different; but Lindley, who for recreation had jumped across Peck Slip (twenty-one feet!) and had become injured in some such athletics, went to England on account of poor health. Becoming little better, he settled at Holdgate, and died there, leaving a residue of his property as a permanent fund the income from which was to be used "in liberating black people who may be held in Slavery, assisting them when freed, and in giving their descendants suitable education; in promoting the civilization and instruction of the Indians of North America; in the purchase and distribution of books tending to promote piety & Virtue & the truth of Christianity. And it is my wish, that the 'Power of Religion on the Mind, in Retirement, Affliction, and at the Approach of Death,' with the Author's last

Corrections and improvements may form a considerable part of those books." More than 100,000 copies of this book have been put in circulation since his death; it went through many editions during his life. It was the first of his many books. His *Grammar, Reader, Speller*, etc., followed. His grammar, published in 1792, was long in use in English and American schools, and acknowledged the foremost authority in England and America until superseded by that of Goold Brown. He had been a member of the Manumission Society, and active in the Public School Society. A good portrait may be seen in the *History of the Public School Society*, p. 480.

John Murray, Jr. (1758-1819) another son of Robert, a merchant and philanthropist, is considered in connection with the Public School Society, which he was active in establishing.

Robert I. Murray (1786-1856) son of John, Jr., was a wealthy druggist, one of the governors of the New York Hospital from 1816 until his death, forty-two years later, and was for thirty-four years Secretary to the Board. He was a Manager of the House of Refuge until he resigned in 1853, a Manager of the Institution for the Blind until his death, and for some years a Director of the Bank of North America.

Goold Brown (1791-1857) was the son of a Quaker school teacher of Providence, Rhode Island. He could read Greek when five years old. His later education was acquired in the Moses Brown School, established at Providence in 1819 by New England Yearly Meeting, and lately given its present name in honor to the memory of him whose generosity and foresight made it possible. Goold Brown was a teacher for some time in the Nine Partners Boarding School, a Yearly Meeting school in Dutchess County, N. Y. He then opened an Academy in this city in 1812, which he conducted for twenty years, and which was noted for its classical and literary training. He first published his *Grammar* in 1823, and it was a "best seller" for many years, being used in the public schools of this city until 1900. His *Grammar of Grammars*, published in 1851, after twenty-three years' work thereon is "the most exhaustive, most accurate, and most original treatise on the English language ever written." (*Nat. Cyclopedia of Am. Biography*, VIII, 265.) The "Lexicographer's Chair" in the *Literary Digest* still frequently cites it as authority.

George Fox Cooledge, who came in 1821 with his parents from the Monthly Meeting of Weare, New Hampshire, became a publisher of school books, including Noah Webster's *Spelling Book* when that was the most popular book of its kind in America. He was interested in various Philanthropies. The Register of Members shows that Twentieth Street Monthly Meeting disowned him in 1843, but the minutes show nothing relative to this or to several other disownments of that period.

Isaac T. Hopper (1771-1852) Abolitionist and bookseller, whose name is now perhaps better known than that of any other Quaker of this city, is considered in connection with "Discipline."

Mahlon Day (-1855) removed from Burlington, N. J., in 1813. He was for many years in the printing and bookselling business, and published some works of his own. Among these were *The American Infant School Primer*, and *Tariff, or rates of duties . . . for the direction of merchants*. It appears to be this latter which was one of the required text books in the Friends' Institute, noted under "Education." See further reference under "Public School System." In 1855 he obtained a minute of unity with his concern to pay a religious visit to meetings in England and Ireland. The steamship *Arctic* was lost at sea, and he and his family were among those who perished.

Samuel Wood (1760-1844) was born in the Town of Oyster Bay, Long Island, and christened in the Episcopalian Church there, but joined Friends early in life. He taught school in various localities, and removed to New York City in 1803, opening a book store the following year at 362 Pearl Street. He soon added a printing plant and began publishing. Observing the poor quality of books printed for children, he set out to fill the need. His first publication was *The Young Child's A B C, or First Book*, of sixteen pages about three inches square, written by himself. Other similar books followed, most of them with copperplate illustrations. He was in the habit of carrying his pockets full of these to give to children. In 1810, he brought out the first American edition of Fox's *Book of Martyrs,* with a list of over four thousand subscribers. His series of school readers included *The New York Primer, The New York Preceptor, The New York Spelling-Book* and *The New York Expositor.* He published *Wood's Almanac* from 1811 to 1834. In 1836 he disposed of his interest to his sons and devoted his remaining years to philanthropy. He was actively associated with the Bank for Savings, the Society for the Prevention of Pauperism, the House of Refuge, the Manumission Society, and the Society of the New York Hospital. Observing the prevalence of opthalmia among children of the poor, he appealed to the public through the newspapers. Dr. Samuel Akerly espoused the cause, and to the exertions of these two is the city indebted for the Institution for the Blind. A good portrait of this good man is given on page 35 of *John Wood of Attercliffe, Yorkshire, England . . . and his Descendants,* by Arnold Wood, 1903, from which this account is taken.

William Wood (1797-1877) son of Samuel. He was admitted into his father's firm in 1822. He was much interested in medicine, and developed what is now the principal business of the firm. He was one of the founders of the Mercantile Library. He was Clerk of Twentieth Street Yearly Meeting for several years. He had a care for the preservation of the records, and indexed a number of them. His portrait is on page 47 of the above mentioned book.

William H. S. Wood (1840-1907) son of William, was admitted to partnership in 1865, the firm name being then changed to its present form of William Wood & Co., and built up the business to be the first in the line of medical publishers in this country. He was a trustee of the Bowery Savings Bank, a Manager of the New York Bible Society, a director of the Young Men's Christian Association, and president of the Bowery Savings Bank from 1903 till his death. His brochure, *Friends of the City of New York in the Nineteenth Century,* 1904, has helped much in relation to some of the names and facts in this chapter.

Israel Corse (1769-1842) is said to have been born in Maryland, and to have run away from home and stepfather at the age of seventeen, apprenticing himself to a tanner in Camden, Delaware, where, on completion of his service, he had a capital of seventy-five cents. In the next ten years he appears to have acquired a livelihood, a wife and family, and to have lost several children. (*Old Merchants of New York* I, 253.) When he became a member of meeting is not clear, but in 1803 he brought a removal certificate for himself, wife Lydia and son Barney from Murderkiln Monthly Meeting, Delaware. He made a fortune as a tanner and dealer in hides in the "Swamp"—that section on the lower east side of the city which is still so called in memory of its boggy past. He was a member of the Manumission Society, and subscribed a double amount for life membership in the Society for the reformation of Juvenile Delinquents when that society established the House of Refuge in 1824. Like Thomas Eddy he was a good lobbyist, and secured the passage by the State Legislature of a law which made the selling of lottery tickets a crime. Unless we study the matter of the lotteries of a century ago we cannot well comprehend to what an evil they had grown, to what an extent their influence permeated society, and to what extent we are indebted to Israel Corse. He retired from business in 1830. His tannery was on Jacob Street, near where, in 1826, a "mineral spring" was discovered, the water from which sold at sixpence a drink and worked a number of cures—until it was found to be supplied through old and forgotten tan vats!

Barney Corse (-1878) son of Israel, continued the leather business of his father for two years, in partnership with Jonathan Thorne, who had married his sister; he then retired.

Jonathan Thorne (1801-1884) continued the leather business of his father-in-law until his death.

Joseph A. Scoville, under the pseudonym of "Walter Barrett," in his gossipy (but not always accurate) *Old Merchants of New York* relates more about these three wealthy men, Israel, Barney and Jonathan. The tradition of their generosity still lives in the Quaker circle. Jonathan was a Director of the Society for the Prevention of Cruelty to Children from its organization till his death.

George T. Trimble (1793-1872) born of Quaker parents in Chester County, Pa., removed to this city in 1809. His firm, Byrnes, Trimble and Company, established the Red Star line of packet ships to Europe in 1822. He was a trustee of the Public School Society from 1818 to 1853, and was President from 1847 to 1853, when that society gave over its work. He was a Governor of the New York Hospital, a trustee of the Roosevelt Hospital, and Clerk of New York Yearly Meeting at Fifteenth Street. For further data see *Descendants of John and Mary Palmer*, 1875, where a portrait is given. A better portrait is in the *History of the Public School Society*, p. 320.

Elias Hicks, Jr. (1815-1853), was a grandson of the noted minister. His father, Valentine Hicks, placed him as an apprentice in this city in 1833. He later became so successful and energetic in the ship chandlery business that he was elected president of the New York Chamber of Commerce in 1853, probably the youngest ever chosen for that position, which was an honor sought and prized by merchants of the city. He held the office but a few months, dying of tuberculosis. It should be stated, for clarity, that his mother was Abigail Hicks, daughter of the preacher, of whom Valentine was a nephew.

Benjamin Tatham, Jr. (-1885) brought his certificate from Hitchin Monthly Meeting, in Hertfordshire, England, in 1841. He had a shot tower, on Beekman Street, but during the Civil War, felt it not right to make shot, and made only lead pipe till the end of that conflict. Meanwhile he actively represented the Society of Friends at Washington, but declined the Commissionership of Indian Affairs, although urged by President Lincoln to accept it. (Again the avoidance of "profit or honor.") His shot tower, long a notable part of the scenery from the Brooklyn Bridge, was demolished in 1923. His wife was Rebecca Collins, granddaughter of Isaac Collins, also granddaughter of Robert Bowne, both elsewhere mentioned.

James C. Hallock (1809-1885) was the father of the New York Clearing House, though himself not a banker. In 1852 he proposed arbitration between the banks of New York in the form of a Clearing House. The bankers would not consider the London plan, whereupon he invented an original method, the most expeditious ever devised, and persuaded the bankers to adopt it. The Clearing House was opened October 11, 1853, since which there has been peace and harmony between the banks. Theretofore the banks of this city had kept accounts with each other, Friday being the regular settlement day, and had been periodically in a state of private war by forcing settlements with certain banks on other days. The philanthropies and charities instituted or assisted by certain Friends might have been so begun or carried on by any open-minded, open-hearted Quaker of means and opportunity, but his was the creative brain which had the vision and which made it real, to whom is due the simplification of trade and the safety and convenience of everyone who makes use of a bank. This has reduced the cost of exchange, and added in a large degree to the stability of banks. He was not a banker; he derived no reward from this contribution. I wonder if there are now ten bank presidents who know the name of James C. Hallock?

The Chamber of Commerce was established in 1768, the pioneer organization, and has been maintained on the town meeting system of open action, openly arrived at, by the members in attendance at a meeting. It has adjusted maritime and trade disputes from the beginning. Robert Murray and Walter Franklin were among the incorporators; John Murray was president 1798-1806, and Elias Hicks (the younger) for part of 1852, until his death; each of these having previously been vice president for several years; William Shotwell was secretary 1786-1787.

The Bank for Savings in the City of New York, the first Savings Bank in the city, was opened in 1819. Thomas Eddy and John Murray, Jr., were on the first Board of Trustees, and John Murray, Jr., was vice president. Five of its twenty-four Directors were Quakers.

The Bowery Savings Bank was chartered in 1834. Among the Quakers in the corporation were Edward Wood (-1894) president 1880 to 1894; John D. Hicks (1831-1907) president 1899 to 1903; William H. S. Wood (1840-1907), president 1903 to 1907; and the following trustees, with year of appointment: John Carle, Jr., 1852; Robert H. Haydock, 1852; John D. Hicks, 1858; Robert Haydock, 1862; William H. S. Wood, 1872; John T. Willets, 1879; David S. Taber, 1884. John D. Hicks, who had been second and then first vice president, and was the senior member of the board, on taking the office of president asked and secured a resolution by the board "to make his salary conform to the sum that he has been willing to take, which was considerably less than was paid to his predecessor." (*Manual of the Bowery Savings Bank*, 1903, p. 91.) He was a member of this Monthly Meeting for several years, but returned to Westbury Monthly Meeting in 1863. Samuel B. Haines was a teller in this bank for many years.

The New York Hospital, the first in the city, was established in 1770. Thomas Eddy was eighth President, 1822 to 1827; George Thomas Trimble was eleventh President, 1858 to 1872; William Henry Macy was fourteenth President, 1882 to 1887; Merritt Trimble, son of George T., was seventeenth President, 1891 to 1897; David Colden Murray, son of Robert I., was Secretary, 1858 to 1885; Valentine Seaman was attending surgeon, 1796 to 1817; Valentine Mott followed him, till 1837; John C. Chee   was attending surgeon, 1821 to 1856. Thomas Cock and his son Thomas Ferris Cock were attending physicians for many years.

The first State Prison was built in 1796, and opened (closed is a better word) in 1797. It was on Greenwich Street, extending to the river, about a block from Christopher Street Ferry, but it was then over two miles from the city. The distinctive terra cotta plaque in the subway station at Christopher and Varick Streets (these being different in each station) gives a conventionalized view of this prison, which remained in use for half a century. The plan and front elevation are shown in *An Account of the State Prison or penitentiary house in the city of New York,* 1801, written by Thomas Eddy. Several Quakers were on the building commission, and the work was under the personal supervision of Thomas Eddy, "the Howard of America" of whom more is told elsewhere, and whose persistent lobbying at Albany had secured the establishment of this improved prison. The ground (four acres) and buildings cost $208,-

ooo. In the *Life of Thomas Eddy*, p. 19, is given a letter to the author from Cadwallader D. Colden, former Lieutenant Governor, and then Assistant Attorney General, which states "that the members of the first board of governors of the State Prison were mostly taken from the society of Friends," and that Thomas Eddy was Superintendent. "The good order, comfort, cleanliness, industry, and devotion which prevailed, as long as the Friends had the management of the institution, were very remarkable." But in 1800 a landslide election brought the prison into political patronage and the Quakers were soon out. The new management was so bad that it very nearly caused the failure of this great experiment, for the prison had been a great step in advance of former penal institutions. The Report of the Inspectors of the State Prison dated "1st Month 15th, 1799" is signed by Isaac Stoutenburgh, Robert Bowne,* Thomas Eddy,* John Murray, Jr.,* Jotham Post, George Warner, Thomas Franklin.* The Report dated "2nd Month 11th, 1803" is signed by Robert Bowne,* John Murray, Jr.,* Thos. Franklin,* Geo. Warner, Leonard Bleecker, Thomas Eddy,* W. Few. The Report dated February 10, 1804, is signed by William W. Gilbert, Leonard Bleecker, John Bingham, Robert Bowne,* George Warner, Thomas Eddy.* Those whose names are starred were members of New York Monthly Meeting. The first of these reports is couched in "Friendly" language. That of 1804 states that "Though the zeal of its Inspectors has heretofore prompted them, for the promotion of the interests of the prison, to advance large sums of money individually, it cannot be expected that they should continue such advances." They also report with regret, that twenty of the prisoners had recently tried to scale the walls and escape, with a result that four were killed by the guards. I think we may read between the lines that no escape had been undertaken while the prison was under Quaker control.

The first regular line of packet ships between this port and Liverpool was the Black Ball Line, established in 1817 by Francis Thompson (1772-1832), Jeremiah Thompson (1784-1835) and Isaac Wright and son, all Quakers. They owned the four ships with which the line began—the *Pacific*, the *Amity*, the *Courier* and the *James Monroe*. The *Amity* was built in 1816 by Forman Cheeseman, a member of this meeting, and the *Courier* in 1817 by Sidney Wright, a nephew of Isaac Wright. These ships were of about 400 tons burthen. Benjamin Marshall, not known to be a Quaker but whose wife was buried in the Friends' cemetery, was also an owner. There had been independent packet ships making fairly regular sailings at long intervals, since 1780, but this line, later with eight ships, and with fine passenger accommodations made regular semi-monthly sailings. Their distinguishing mark was a large black ball

A Black Ball Liner of 1826
From the painting by Charles Robert Patterson

painted on the foretopsail. Jeremiah was considered to be the largest importer in America of British cloths, and an exporter of cotton to Liverpool, but does not appear to have felt the need of advertising. Francis was more closely engaged in the shipping business. *Old Merchants of N. Y.* by Joseph A. Scoville, under the Pseudonym of "Walter Barrett," gives additional information of the Thompsons. The Line, still in great prestige, passed into the ownership of Jonathan Goodhue & Co. in 1834. Jeremiah Thompson was Clerk of the Monthly Meeting for ten years, 1814-1824.

Another line of packets, the Red Star line, was established in 1821 or 1822, by Byrnes, Trimble & Company, the Junior partner being George T. Trimble, who is further referred to in other chapters. Samuel Hicks, a Quaker merchant, was interested in this line. Thomas Shipley Byrnes, born in Wilmington, Delaware, brought his certificate from Cornwall Monthly Meeting, Orange County. Associated with them was Silas Wood, eldest son of Samuel Wood, a flour merchant of Fredericksburg, Va., though born on Long Island. After Byrnes' death, at sea, 1825, Silas Wood returned to New York and the firm became Wood and Trimble. Silas is described as a "Demi-Quaker" in a pamphlet of 1845, *Wealth and Biography of the Wealthy Citizens of New York*, 2d ed., 1845, but was not a member, having joined the Episcopalian Church.

Another line was established by Preserved Fish and Joseph Grinnell, both from New Bedford. Fish withdrew about 1826, and was succeeded by Robert Bowne Minturn, a grandson of Robert Bowne. R. B. Minturn was reared a Friend, but later joined the Episcopalian Church. (*Memoir of Robert Bowne Minturn*, 1871.)

The first Gas Company in the city was organized in 1825, or at least it lighted the first house that year. Samuel F. Leggett, a wealthy and prominent Quaker, was president, and it was his residence, No. 7 Cherry Street, which was first lighted. Other houses soon followed, but for some time only the parlors were lighted by gas, candles and oil being retained for other rooms.

Valentine's Manual for 1855, p. 563, states the value, at the beginning of the nineteenth century, of several fine houses occupied in part by stores, such buildings being considered the most valuable property in the city. Among these I find the following Quakers: Thomas Eddy, $7,000, John Murray, $15,000, Pearsall and Bowne, $10,000, Edmund Prior, $15,000, Thomas Pearsall and Son, $9,000.

The annals of the volunteer Fire Companies would show many Quaker names, but I have not compiled them. I was told by an old Friend (Henry Carpenter) who had been a member of one of these, how he, and other firemen, laid aside their clothing at night in a particular manner with great care, so that dressing might be done in the least possible time, although such disposition of the clothing sadly wrinkled it; and how the leather fire buckets, and the glossy hat, so different from the "plain" one of every day, occupied a prominent place by the front door.

Among Quakers of less note may be mentioned the following: John Clapp (1781-1857) a flour merchant at 242 Front Street, became president of the Mechanics and Traders Bank in 1837 and held that position until his death twenty years later. A daughter Phebe married Richard Henry Thomas, of Baltimore; a grandson, Allan Clapp Thomas, was a professor at Haverford College and a Quaker historian; a great grandson is a member at Twentieth Street, which brings the line back to New York. One of the long list of Quaker whalers of Nantucket was Thomas Hazard, who after making a fortune in that industry increased it in trade in this city. David Sands (— -1859) was a wholesale druggist, and the wealthiest Quaker of his day. He was at one time the teacher in the school maintained by Twentieth Street Friends. John B. Lawrence, another wealthy Quaker and wholesale druggist was at 195 Pearl Street about 1794. Samuel Willets (1795-1883) and his brother Robert R. (1802-1879) established as Willets and Company, a hardware business in 1815. Samuel Willets was a member of the Manumission Society, and a Director of the Society for the Prevention of Cruelty to Children. The late John T. Willets, and his brothers Robert R. and William, sons of the elder Robert R., continued the firm of Willets and Company, then a general commission house. I think the business was always at No. 303 Pearl Street, until the death of John T. Willets. John T. Willets was a manager of Swarthmore College and Vice President of the Society for the Relief of the Ruptured and Crippled. He was Treasurer of the Hahneman Hospital, the New York Infirmary for Women and Children, the Martha Scofield School and other philanthropies. Samuel Willets gave a large endowment to Swarthmore College.

Gideon Frost (1798-1880) brought his certificate from Westbury in 1824, and returned to that meeting in 1843. He established by legacy the Friends' Academy at Locust Valley, Long Island, now a justly flourishing school, fitting the students for Life, and incidently for college. John D. Wright (1799-1879) devout Friend and earnest minister, is mentioned in connection with the Society for the Prevention of Cruelty to Children. His son, John Howard Wright (1828-1915) straightened nails as his first job, and his last job was as Secretary of the Standard Oil Trust during the decade of its existence, after which he became an active retired business man, whose careful writing as Recorder of the vital data, and whose hearty courtesy are remembered by many. Joseph A. Bogardus (1851-1896) sold hardware as a vocation; for avocation he spent himself in religious and philanthropic work. His life and activities have remained an inspiration to the writer. He was one of the original members of the Young Friends' Aid Association, and very active in it until his death. William M. Jackson (1833-1919) came from Richmond, Indiana, where he had taught evolution in Friends' School. He became Assistant Principal of Friends' Seminary, and was chairman of the board for twenty-five years. He was one of the first among Friends to make a scientific study of the Bible.

The following is a list of the Clerks of New York Yearly Meeting, those starred being members of New York Monthly Meeting. Before 1763 the clerk is not named in the minutes. The dates are inclusive.

* Edward Burling, 1763-1774.
* George Bowne, 1775, 1787-1789, 1793-1797.
* Oliver Hull, 1776, 1778-1779.
   William Rickman, 1777.
   Silas Downing, 1780-1783.
* Edmund Prior, 1784-1786.
   James Mott, 1790-1792.
* Richard Mott, 1798, 1801-1803, 1807, 1809-1816 (see below).
* John Murray, Jr., 1799-1800, 1804-1806.
* John Barrow, 1808.
* Samuel Parsons, 1817-1828 (see below).

Twentieth Street Yearly Meeting

* Samuel Parsons, 1828-1841.

*Richard Mott, 1842-1850 (same individual as above).
Richard Carpenter, 1851-1856.
*William Wood, 1857-1867, 1869-1870.
*Stephen Wood, 1868.
*Robert L. Murray, 1871-1874.
*Augustus Taber, 1875-1881, 1883-1890.
*Charles H. Jones, 1891-1893.
James Wood, 1882, 1894-1925.
L. Hollingsworth Wood, 1926-1930.

Fifteenth Street Yearly Meeting

*Samuel Mott, 1828-1830.
Stephen Underhill, 1831-1839.
Thomas Wright, 1840-1846.
*Samuel Willets, 1847-1852.
*George T. Trimble, 1853-1863.
*Nathaniel S. Merritt, 1864-1871, 1875-1879.
*Charles A. Macy, 1872-1874.
Robert S. Haviland, 1880-1888.
*William H. Willits, 1889-1908.
James S. Haviland, 1909-1914.
Ellwood Burdsall, 1915-1930.
Edward Cornell appointed for 1931.

Women's Yearly Meeting

Clerk not named before 1775

Margaret Dobson, 1775.
Eleanor Moode, 1776.
Anne Willis, 1777, 1789-1792.

* Hannah Haydock, 1778-1788.
* Hannah Pearsall, 1793-1795.
* Amy Bowne, 1796.
  Hannah Cornell, 1797.
  Phebe Downing, 1798-1799, 1801-1802.
* Elizabeth Bowne, 1800.
* Anne Mott, 1803, 1805-1807, 1809-1813, 1815-1817.
* Anna Merritt   } 1804, 1808.
* Anna Merritt Thorne } 1814.
* Abigail Evernghim   } 1818-1821.
* Abigail E. Thurston } 1822-1823, 1825-1828 (see below).
  Anna M. Willis, 1824.

Twentieth Street Yearly Meeting

* Anne Mott, 1828-1831.
  Anna W. Willis, 1832.
* Sarah Waring, 1833-1838.
  Elizabeth (Underhill) Willis, 1839-1860.
  Maria Willets, 1861-1872.
* Caroline E. Ladd, 1881-1884.
        (after which joint sessions)

Fifteenth Street Yearly Meeting

  Mary Bristol, 1828-1829.
* Ann M. Comstock, 1830-1842.
* Abigail E. Thurston, 1843-1844, 1846-1849.
* Mary U. Hicks, 1845.
* Deborah M. Field, 1850-1851.
  Hannah H. Frost, 1852-1856.

Rachael Hicks, 1857-1866.
Mary Jane Field, 1867-1882.
* Amanda K. Miller, 1883-1888.
* Jane W. Carpenter, 1889-1893.
Emily P. Yeo, 1894-1903.
    (after which joint sessions)

The individuals mentioned in this chapter, members of one or the other meeting, are representative of many others now forgotten, whose lives and works have served mankind beyond their plain and manifest duty—who have gone "the second mile"—who have in their several ways made this city a better city because of their life in it.

I have herein written of men, and of men almost solely. None can doubt that there were many women who labored as earnestly and efficiently as the men in all good works, and especially in behalf of women and children. They have in all periods been active in relieving want and suffering, in nursing the sick and mothering the orphaned. The sole reason I have not told more concerning them is that I have not learned their names, their deeds having been done in quiet ways, unnoted by the world. They did not get into the public eye or come under the biographer's notice. Reflection shows this state of things to be common to other organizations, and indeed to all history. The work of the Female Association, considered under "Education," shows how numerous were the women willing and earnest in such a cause. Under "Philanthropy and Charity" is noted the women who established the Employment Society, and those who helped to organize the Young Friends' Aid Association and the Friendly Hand. Among prominent women members known to the writer was the late Mariana W. Chapman, active in every reform, in touch with leaders of social and political thought. The reform she had perhaps most at heart—equal suffrage—was accomplished after her death, but she had helped to bring it to pass. Another philanthropist and reformer was Anna M. Jackson. Her special field was the education of Negroes in the South, but she found time for many other philanthropies, and was president of the Young Friends' Aid Association for thirty-five years. For a score of years she was interested in the Police system of the City. Her advice was frequently sought by the Commissioners. The acquisition of wealth weakened the Quakerism of some members, but one great exception to this was the late Phebe Anna Thorne, daughter of Jonathan Thorne, whose quiet benefactions can never be forgotten by those who helped her disburse them, and who became ever a better Friend as her fortune increased. By her bequest was established in 1910 the Phebe Anna Thorne School for Girls, under the direction of the Department of Education of Bryn Mawr College.

This is not the place in which to discuss the causes and general effects on the whole Society of Friends, of the withdrawal—the shirking of certain important duties of citizenship—in avoiding political office, which is shown in this chapter. It is with the effect of it on Quakerism as lived and practised in this city that we are now concerned. The number of Quakers remained small to the end of the Colonial period, there being in 1782 not over fifty-eight "of suitable age" to serve on the watch, as elsewhere noted. This was in a city of about 23,000. In the general expansion which followed the establishment of the Union, of which the increase in population is an index, and when new meetings were settled throughout the State in a continuous progression, the Society in this city increased rapidly, there being a continuous influx of members by certificate from country meetings. By 1830 the City had a population of 202,000, although still "watched" at night, the Police system not beginning till the 40s. The list of Friends, showing which side each took in the lamentable Separation of 1828, gives a total of 1,832 in this Monthly Meeting. This is probably the maximum number of Friends in this city, and from that unfortunate date the divided Society rapidly diminished.

The Quakers had acquired since they became established here, the esteem of their neighbors, the good will of the entire city, and a number had acquired wealth. They were ready in every good work —or nearly ready, for their inherent conservatism delayed them on some reforms. In education, in manumission, in certain philanthropies, they led. But it was only after he had left the Society that Walter Bowne, descendant of John the banished, became the only Quaker Mayor and successor of Stuyvesant the banisher. They persisted in declining "posts of profit or honor," and dealt with members who accepted such. This shrinking into a shell is a part of that narrowness of mind and atrophy of soul which allowed and created the Separation. Yet throughout this long period Quakerism had produced, not only many saintly lives and effective preachers, but a good and increasing number of men of high intelligence and fair education, well qualified for participation in the civic affairs of the city, State and nation. It is well that under this hampering influence they turned to what they could of amelioration of suffering and of overcoming of evil by good.

Quaker Doctors

The list of physicians and surgeons, members of this meeting, would be longer had we all the names of those who have worthily followed their honorable calling. The list begins with Dr. John Rodman (1653-1731) of Flushing. He was born of Quaker parents in Barbados, where in 1679 he owned forty-seven acres of valuable land and thirteen slaves. He was fined 1,350 pounds of sugar "for default of appearing in the Troop." He removed to Newport, Rhode Island, about 1682, and to Flushing about 1691. He was admitted a freeman in New York City in 1698, and was a resident of this city as early as 1695, owning land on the East River and on Crown (now Liberty) Street. "Rodman's Slip," shown on old maps, was later called Burling Slip. The tax list for 1699 shows his houses and property assessed at £420. Only Frederick Phillipse and the merchant, and former Mayor, Gabriel Minveile, were assessed for greater wealth in the entire city, which already included the Harlem ward, eight miles away. The record of deaths states that he was "an eminent doctor, did abundance of good in that practice, and was also a worthy minister of the gospel in this town about 40 years, a man beloved by all sorts of people, lived to a good old age, about 78 years, died ye 10 day of 7 mo 1731." A memorial of him states that "He was very serviceable to friends, and all people that came to him in the way of his business, which was Phisick & Surgery and would greatly deny himself in leaving his company, when going to or coming from Meeting and has, contrary to expectation or inclination, gone in a cross to his own mind to see some ailing body believing it was well to be serviceable in his Generation that he might give no occasion to any to be offended at Friends." See *Genealogy of the Rodman Family,* 1886, for additional data.

Thomas Rodman, elder brother of Dr. John Rodman, was an eminent physician, and the first Clerk of New England Yearly Meeting. He was never a member of this Monthly Meeting.

John Rodman, Jr. (1679-1756) son of Dr. John Rodman, was a practising physician. He was admitted a freeman at Newport in 1706, and removed in 1712 to Flushing, where he resided until 1726, when he removed to New Jersey. He occupied many public offices in New Jersey, and owned thirteen hundred acres there and a large tract in Bucks County, Pennsylvania, which he acquired in 1712.

I have not learned who the Dr. Robinson was, whose Scotch servant received relief from the meeting in 1688, mentioned under "Philanthropy."

The next one I have learned of is Valentine Seaman (1770-1817) who was a pupil of the famous Dr. Benjamin Rush of Philadelphia. He was the first to institute clinical lectures in the New York Hospital, in 1801, and was the first to analyze the waters of Saratoga Springs, writing an exhaustive treatise on their use. The record of deaths for 1796 shows a sad and large list of children's names, including "Valentine Seaman's child," probably from the smallpox epidemic of that year. His reaction to the loss of his first born was a voyage to England and consultation with Dr. Jenner, with the result that Dr. Seaman introduced vaccination here. He was the first to have a class for instruction in midwifery, and wrote a book for the guidance of practitioners. He was an active member of the Manumission Society. Rembrandt Peale's portrait of him in 1816 shows him the courteous, alert minded, ideally professional doctor, inspiring confidence. Wilson's *Memorial History of New York*, IV, 398-399, has a woodcut of this, and some account of his life.

Dr. James V. Seaman (1799- ?) son of Dr. Valentine Seaman, graduated in 1817 from the College of Physicians and Surgeons. He was disowned for "marrying out" in 1824, and so lost to the Society.

Dr. Valentine Seaman (1802-1899) another son of the first named was disowned. He was a successful practitioner, and father of a still more noted Surgeon Major-General.

Thus did a rigid adherence to the Discipline drive out of the Society a line of humanity-helpers. A far cry from the spirit of the Paper of Advice of Fox.

Dr. Shadrach Ricketson (1766-1839) who had been for several years clerk of Creek Monthly Meeting, in Dutchess County, brought his removal certificate to New York in 1806, and published a 300 page book that year on *Means of Preserving Health and Preventing Disease,* which was commended by Valentine Seaman and six other physicians of this city. He practised medicine and surgery here until 1812, when he began his numerous removals, to Easton, Troy, Oswego, Nine Partners, and in 1821 again to his birthplace, in Oswego Monthly Meeting in Dutchess County. He had probably studied medicine with some physician in his vicinity, perhaps in Poughkeepsie. He published a map of all meetings in the Yearly Meeting in 1821, showing the mileage between meetings. He bequeathed legacies to several Monthly Meetings for schools.

John Cummings Cheeseman (1787-1862) was a pupil of Valentine Seaman, and graduated at Queens (now Rutgers) College in 1812. He was for forty years connected with the New York Hospital, was President of the New York County Medical Society in 1842, and was considered one of the most eminent physicians in the United States.

Timothy Matlack Cheeseman (1824-   ) son of John C. Cheeseman, graduated from the College of

Physicians and Surgeons in 1859, and was a member of the County Society and of the Academy of Medicine.

Timothy Matlack Cheeseman, Jr., son of above, became Assistant Professor in the College of Physicians and Surgeons in 1900. He was not a member of meeting, his father and grandfather both having been disowned before his birth. Portraits of all three are in *Portraits of the noted Physicians of New York, 1750-1900*, by W. G. Eliot, 1900.

Dr. Henry Mott (1757-1839) practised in this city for many years. His house was at 259 Pearl Street for many years, but his last residence was at 545 Broadway. I have learned nothing further about him.

Valentine Mott (1785-1865), son of Dr. Henry, was a pupil of his kinsman, Valentine Seaman, and graduated from Columbia College in 1806. He then went to London and became a pupil of Sir Astley Cooper, attended lectures by the chief masters of surgery there, and was at Edinburgh University more than a year. Returning in 1809, he was made professor of surgery at Columbia College in 1810. On one of his European tours he was decorated by the Sultan for removing a tumor from the head of the latter. He was the principal founder of the New York University Medical College in 1841, and president of the faculty. He was thereafter at various periods surgeon to the New York, Bellevue, St.

Luke's, St. Vincent's, Hebrew and Women's hospitals. The list is long of delicate surgical operations which he was the first to perform, all duly set forth in an article in the *National Cyclopedia of American Biography*, VI, 281, where also a good portrait is reproduced. He received degrees from colleges, and was made a fellow of several foreign chirurgical societies, was long president of the New York Academy of Medicine, and was president of the Inebriate Asylum. Two sons and a grandson followed in his footsteps, but as he was disowned in 1825, he and they were lost to the Society. The charge against him was "for attendance of a place of diversion and neglecting attendance of our religious meetings." He admitted being "remiss" in attending meeting "owing to the multiplicity of business, but he did not consider that he had attended a place of diversion." In 1847 he was able for a little time to help the unfortunate Edgar Allan Poe recover from his "nightmare of sorrows," according to Hervey Allen in *Israfel*.

Alexander B. Mott (1826-   ) fifth child of Dr. Valentine Mott, was an eminent and able surgeon. He was not a member, owing to the previous disownment of his father. See Francis' *Sketches of Living N. Y. Surgeons*, 1866, p. 105, for further data.

Dr. William Seaman (1792-1855) brought his certificate from Jericho Monthly Meeting, Long Island, in 1828. It is probable that he began his studies in the office of his near kinsman, Dr. Valentine Seaman.

He graduated from Rutgers College in 1827, and became a member of the County Medical Society in 1832. He had a happy personality and high standing as a physician. He was particularly successful in his treatment of cholera in the epidemic of 1832, losing only two patients from that disorder. One of these was already *in extremis;* the other was 72 years of age.

Dr. Thomas Cock (1783-1869) was a Quaker, who does not appear to have been a member of this meeting, but deserves mention. He was probably a member of Westbury Monthly Meeting. He began the study of medicine in company with Valentine Mott and John C. Cheeseman in the office of Valentine Seaman, and graduated in Columbia College in 1805. He became a partner of Dr. Seaman. During the epidemic of yellow fever in this city in 1822 he was among the most indefatigable and untiring in his efforts to overcome the disease; again during the cholera epidemic in 1832, when his protracted labors and ceaseless devotion were appropriately recognized by the City authorities by the presentation of a service of silver. He was president for three years of the College of Physicians and Surgeons; connected with the New York Hospital for many years; long an active member, and at his death a vice president, of the American Bible Society. A fine portrait of him is reproduced in the Cock-Cocks-Cox Genealogy, p. 58.

Dr. Thomas Ferris Cock (1819-1896) son of Thomas above mentioned, was the first graduate of Haverford School in 1836, before it was called a college, and received the degree of LL.D from that institution, in 1886. He studied medicine in the office of Dr. Alexander Stevens, a prominent surgeon of this City, and in the office of Dr. George B. Wood, of Philadelphia, and graduated from the University of Pennsylvania in 1839. He was consulting physician to the New York Hospital, the Women's Hospital, the Women's Infirmary, and the Lying-in Asylum, and was a trustee of the New York Hospital. The Lying-in Asylum, on Marion Street, incorporated in 1827, was originated largely by his mother, Elizabeth (Ferris) Cock, and he was connected with it for fifty-five years. His portrait is on p. 97 of the above mentioned genealogy. He "married out" in 1842.

James Rushmore Wood, M.D., LL.D. (1813-1882). His parents, Elkanah and Mary, brought a certificate for themselves and him from Mamaroneck (Purchase Monthly Meeting) in 1826. From *American Medical Biographies,* 1920, p. 1257; from *Sketches of Living N. Y. Surgeons,* by Francis, 1866, and other sources, something is learned of this remarkable man. He attended Friends' school on Pearl Street, where he received his early and only academic education, and for three years only. He had, as a boyish hobby, collected and preserved skeletons of small animals. In 1829 he began attending lectures at the College of Physicians and Surgeons, and graduated from the Medical College at Castleton, Vermont, in 1834. He was immediately appointed demonstrator of anatomy, but returned to New York and resumed the practise of medicine in 1837 (having practised here under a license before graduation). He was a great politician and a warm friend of Henry Clay, in later life proudly using on state occasions a cane the latter had given him. That appears to have been his only ostentation. In 1847 he succeeded in getting the almshouse and its so-called hospital at Bellevue taken out of politics and placed under a board of governors. This board appointed him and two other doctors as a medical board, and the Bellevue Hospital we know to-day is the result. He began his clinics in 1847, with an audience of one, and continued them until at his death his Saturday clinics were watched sometimes by nearly a thousand keen observers, and were the medical event of the week. During the first ten years he performed the majority of the operations, and led a reform in practise, nursing and food, which resulted in an estimated saving of six hundred lives in a year. Ambidextrous, bold and confident, he worked so rapidly in the dreadful days before anesthetics, when speed was so vitally important, that he amputated a thigh in nine seconds. He probably had little time for politics, but in 1874 he was prominent in the successful effort to secure from the State legislature the Act to Promote Medical Science, which directed that the bodies of "all vagrants dying unclaimed" be given to hospitals and medical schools for dissection. Theretofore the need had been supplied by the hangman's rope and the grave robber's shovel. He published some pamphlets, but was too busy to write about much of his important work. An engraving of his portrait in the library of the Academy of Medicine, shows a strong, serious face. His collection of skeletons and other post mortem material, begun as a boy, and now known as the Wood Museum, was called by the eminent Dr. Willard Parker the grandest monument ever erected to any surgeon in this country.

William R. Wagstaff, M.D. (1820-   ) was born a member of the meeting. I have learned nothing as to his studies or practise, except that he graduated in 1842 from the College of Physicians and Surgeons, but a brother was named after John Cheeseman, indicating some connection with that noted physician. He published in 1845 *A History of the Society of Friends, compiled from its standard records*, which he dedicated to his mother. This was Part I, confined to Quakerism in Europe. Part II, relating to America, was to follow, if his health served. He soon after took a removal certificate to London, where his mother and her other children also went. He probably heard of the excellent history then being prepared by James Bowden, and so gave up his intention as to Part II. His *History* as well as his name are forgotten among us, but he became a fellow of the Medical Society of London, and published there in 1851 a treatise on the mucous membrane of the throat.

William J. Baner (1821-1885) brought a certificate in 1847 from Springboro, Ohio. He was a visiting physician in Ward's Island Hospital.

Llewellyn Baner, son of William, graduated in 1885 from the College of Physicians and Surgeons, but as his father had "married out" he was lost to the meeting.

Richard Kirk Valentine (1855-1901) after attending Friends' Seminary and Swarthmore College, graduated from the Homœopathic Medical College in 1875. As he could not secure a license until he was twenty-one, he continued his studies in Germany. He was visiting physician, from 1876 until his death, in the Brooklyn Homœopathic Hospital and in the Home for Consumptives.

Stephen Wood (1811-1884) was a member of the meeting, and was married in meeting, but I have learned nothing further regarding him except that he graduated from the College of Physicians and Surgeons in 1833.

Samuel Whitall (-1882) brought a certificate from Philadelphia in 1863. He published several pamphlets on surgical matters in 1868 and 1873. For many years until his death he was the Surgeon in Chief of the Colored Home Hospital—now The Lincoln Hospital. He was greatly beloved by all.

Charles H. Bushong (1856-1903) brought his certificate from Sadsbury, Pa., taught in Friends' Seminary 1881 to 1884 inclusive, and graduated in medicine from the College of Physicians and Surgeons in 1885. He thereafter practised in this city until his failing health required him to seek a drier air, but tuberculosis soon claimed him. He was a member of the County Medical Society and of the New York Academy of Medicine, and was elected a member of the medical department of the University of Colorado in 1901, but was unable to assume the duties of his position. He became a Medical Director of the Mutual Benefit Life Association in 1887, and was a member of the pension examining board during President Harrison's administration. He published a work on gynecology in 1893, and several pamphlets.

Joshua Lindley Barton (1849-1926) was born a member of Farnham Monthly Meeting in the Province of Quebec. He graduated from the College of Physicians and Surgeons, Columbia University, in 1881, and opened an office in New York City where he spent his life in the practise of his profession.

One of his first appointments was that of attending physician at the Demilt Dispensary, and afterwards he was connected with the Out-patient Departments of Bellevue Hospital and the New York

Throat, Nose and Lung Hospital. He was also for many years one of the Medical Examiners of the Provident Life and Trust Co. and connected with several other Life Insurance Companies. In 1882 he was elected a manager of The New York Colored Mission, and the next year became its president. Very soon afterward he offered his free professional services to the suffering poor who came to the Mission. Busy in his profession he was even busier in philanthropies in and out of the Society of Friends, his quiet benefactions, his hidden kindnesses and his ministrations to the physical and spiritual welfare of the Colored people, their gratitude alone his ample reward.

I will here break my self-imposed rule of not mentioning the living (and there are several Quaker doctors practising in this City) by giving the name of Charles MacDowell, who, after practising medicine for twenty-four years, and retiring in 1902, still lectures at the New York Homœopathic Medical College and Flower Hospital, where he has been a member of the faculty forty-seven years. He has been President of the Academy of Medicine. He studied in the Universities of Leipsic and Vienna.

Quakers in Other Professions

The relief of suffering, the amelioration of the ills of mankind—philanthropy, in short—may be accounted as a cause of Quakers so readily entering the medical profession. Other professions do not appear to have appealed to them to any great degree until Architecture and Engineering began to attain the importance they now have. Teachers there were, always, but not college professors, due to a large and sad misapprehension of a great truth. George Fox had emphasized the fact that "Oxford and Cambridge cannot make a minister"; his followers came to feel, as an erroneous corollary, that one educated at such universities could not be an effective minister of the Truth. It took long to outgrow this feeling. I have not learned of any lawyers among our early Friends. Lindley Murray entered that profession, but does not appear to have practised long. Probably the capture of the city by the British troops was the cause of his retiring to Long Island for the duration of their stay, after which his mind turned to authorship, as elsewhere stated. After the Separation of 1828 a suit was tried at Bedford, Westchester County, between the two branches of the Society in that county. None of the lawyers in the case, so far as I have learned, was a Quaker. Had there been Quaker lawyers in either meeting they would undoubtedly have appeared in that trial. The whole trend of Quaker thought was away from settlement of disputes by process of law. It was only in such a cataclysm that they invoked the law. There are now a number of Quakers in the honorable practise of that profession.

Wilson M. Powell (1834-1915) brought his certificate here from Chatham Monthly Meeting in 1861, having studied in Utica under Senator Roscoe Conkling. For fifty-four years he practised his profession honorably, and conscientiously, largely in the care and protection of private estates and public philanthropies. He prepared the legislative enactments for the Police Matron system in New York City and the Bedford Reformatory and the State Farm for Women. He was active in all the Quaker philanthropies and many others. His wife, Sarah Hopper Brown, was a granddaughter of Isaac T. Hopper.

William H. Willits (1843-1909) was in the practise of law for many years. He was also Clerk of Fifteenth Street Yearly Meeting, as elsewhere stated.

Education

Schooling was a private matter in Colonial life, and until well into the Nineteenth Century in New York State. *The New York Public School*, by A. E. Palmer, 1905, states that Elizabeth Cowperthwait, "daughter of a noted preacher," kept a school in Flushing, 1675 to 1681, and that John Urquhart kept a boarding school there in 1690. Hugh and Grace Cowperthwait had no children. Elizabeth was probably his sister. These statements are probably based on items in the accounts of John Bowne, which throw some light on the matter of education in his day. In 1669 he sold white paper to various individuals, including "Houlding, schoolmaster 3 quires 4/6." In 1680 and 1682 he paid Elizabeth Cowperthwait for "schooling & diet for children." "Martha Joanna (aged ten) did begin school on a new acct 23/2/1683 upon agreement for 30 weeks for schooling & what else which is pd for by a red petticoat bot of John Broke."

In 1692 he had an account with John Arcutt, or Arscot, which shows that when the latter came to town John Bowne had delivered "a barrel of boiled cyder to John Harrison for rent," and was to have "one year scoull £1.1.0." Later in that year "to ye schoolmaster by a fat sheep 10/." In 1693 as executor for the estate of William Richardson of Westchester, he paid John Urquhart for "schooling and diet" for the Richardson boys, at the rate of 0.1.3 per week for teaching "writing and cyphering" to two boys, six-pence for week for teaching a third boy to read, and 0.2.6 per month for going to John Rodman's house to teach the same boy reading and writing. Such was the way to learning among the well-to-do. Wealthier families employed a private tutor. Less able parents had to do without, except what little their own time and ability could supply. The Dutch Reformed Church and the Episcopalian Church maintained some sort of sectarian schools from an early period. In the minutes of the Monthly Meeting for 5th of 6th Month (August) 1703, we see "That a School Ma^r being Judged Necessary for ye towne of flushing, it is thought fitt by this meeting yt Samuel Hoyt & ffrancis Doughty Do Seek out for a Convenient piece of Ground to purchase it, & build a School house thereon, for ye use of friends, about Richd Griffin's Lott, uppon the Cross-way, wch is neere ye Center of ye towne." Undoubtedly the committee did as directed, but it was not a common thing for a committee to report having accomplished its work. If it did its work satisfactorily everyone knew it, and no ink need be used to record it (quite ignoring the likelihood of their descendants digging here and there to ascertain a fact so much in evidence to them). In 1709 the teacher offered to bring the school to mid-week meeting. Here again, no more need be said. If he said he would, it could be depended on, and needed no record. I have not learned if this school had a continuous existence. The minutes are silent on the subject through many decades.

Meanwhile there were a few private non-sectarian schools for the patronage of the well-to-do and wealthy. The following advertisement from the *New York Gazette*, August 28, 1732, shows one of this class. "*Grammar, Writing, Arithmetick Vulgar & Decimal, Taught by* William Thurston, *School-Master in* New York, *dwelling at the Corner-House by* Koenties Market, *over against the* Scotch Arms." And this from the *New York Gazette and Post Boy* for September 15, 1755, shows another. "James Wragg, School-Master, . . . Dock-Street . . . teaches Writing, Arithmetick, Merchants Accounts, Navigation, Surveying, Mensuration, Dialing, and Astronomy &c . . . Due Attendance will be given to young Gentlemen and Ladies at their Houses if required . . . N. B. Night School begins this Month."

In 1780 the Yearly Meeting recommended the establishment by each meeting of a school, and the Monthly Meeting in 12th Month appointed a committee for that purpose. Meantime a school house was in use in New York before 1747 as noted above in connection with the Liberty Street meeting house. This school probably continued down to the Revolutionary War, perhaps to 1781, but the Monthly Meeting minutes show no reference to it, and, as elsewhere shown, John Murray, Jr., and Thomas Eddy attended the Quaker Grammar School in Philadelphia about 1770, the latter's parents then living there, but the former undoubtedly being sent there for lack of an equally good Quaker school here at that time. Whatever the educational conditions here at that time, the Monthly Meeting, under date of 11th Month, 1781, sent the following letter to the Two Weeks Meeting in London:

"DEAR FRIENDS:

Our Yearly Meeting for this Province, held at Westbury on Long Island, taking into consideration the expediency of our Youth being properly instructed in useful learning under the Tuition of a sober discreet Friend, recommended the same thro' the Quarter to the Monthly Meetings. And we being impress'd with a like concern well knowing the Importance of a Suitable Education to Society as well as to Individuals, take the Liberty to request the aid & assistance of your Meeting to furnish us as soon as may be convenient, with a young Man, unmarried, a Member of our Society, of an exemplary life and conversation; a very good writer, well vers'd in Arithmetic and with a competent knowledge of English Grammar. To such a one this Meeting will engage to give annually the Sum of £200 Currency or £112.10 Sterling and we will allow him £42 Sterling for his Passage to this City where he will reside. A School House will be furnished him at our Expense but his board and all other expenses he must himself supply. We apprehend his board may at present cost him about £100 Currency or £56.5 Sterling not more. The number of Scholars

Probably about forty. We would not wish to detar him from keeping an evening School, which if he inclines to, the money from thence arising will be a perquisite to himself: but the Money arising from the Scholars taught in the day time will go toward defraying the above expenses.

With much esteem
Your Loving Friends
signed in and on behalf
of said Meeting by

EDMUNDE PRIOR, Clerk."

With only one misspelled word, the above will compare very favorably with the typewritten business letter of to-day, "dictated but not read" by a college honor man. It also tells much as to social conditions of the period and as to the generosity of the salary. In 1781 Thomas Leggett bought a house in Queen Street (now 307 Pearl Street) but did not occupy it for a time, renting it for $32.50 per year (*Old Merchants of New York*, I, 243). The school the new master was to have was probably on Pearl Street, adjoining the meeting house, which had been used as a barrack by the British during the war, and which would (though they knew it not) be kept from Friends' use for yet two full years. The records of the Two Weeks Meeting in London show, under date of Second Month, 4, 1782, this letter copied in full in their minutes, with the appended minute, "Thomas Gould is directed to carry a copy of this minute to the Meeting for Sufferings." The minutes of the latter meeting show, under date of Third Month, 22, 1782, the essential part of the New York letter, the minute closing with the following paragraph, "This meeting being desirous to afford the said Friends all the assistance in its power we recommend the proposition to the notice of Friends in general, and if any suitable person should offer he is requested to correspond on the subject with James Phillips. Signed by order of the meeting, Thos. Gould. . . . James Phillips is desired to send the above minute to the several counties and places." Norman Penney, the Consulting Librarian of Friends' Reference Library, London, who furnished this information, adds that the Meeting for Sufferings did not record within the next five years, any other minute relative to this matter, and that in the collection of letters of James Phillips no mention is found of a school master for New York.

In 10th Month, 1784, it appears a School is opened in New York, under the Care and direction of the Preparative Meeting there, which hath been attended with a good Degree of Satisfaction, but that no way opens as yet for the establishment of one in the other Preparative Meeting (that of Flushing).

In 4th Month, 1788, the Preparative Meeting of New York reports to the Monthly Meeting as follows: "that they have received from the trustees of the School under their direction encouragement to hope for a material advantage to the rising generation if the Institution continues to be cared for with a perseverance equal to the Import of its object, and further add for the encouragement of their Brethren, that finding the rates of Schooling inadequate to the necessary Salary for a Tutor, qualifyed for this so great a Confidence, a Subscription was opened, by their direction then for a permanent fund the Subscribers paying an annual Interest of five per Cent, to be at Liberty to discharge the Principal, when most easy and agreeable to them, the readiness with which Friends went into this subscription has already Carried the Amount beyond their expectations and affords Relief." This fund amounted to £2121, some of which appears to have been paid off as late as twenty-five years afterward. Meantime the interest was annually paid. Robert Murray bequeathed £200 in 1786 as a perpetual fund for the Friends' School "lately set up in the city."

In 4th Month, 1789, the Preparative Meeting again reports: "that by a Report from the Trustees of the School under its care it appears, that in the Course of their Monthly Visitation they have had to view with Satisfaction an improvement in the Scholars which encourages them to hope not only for a Continuance therein but that an increasing usefulness will result from the institution."

This school was at Pearl Street until 1826, when the larger school house on Elizabeth Street adjoining the Hester Street meeting house, was built. In

1794 children were admitted at the age of seven. Boys were retained until fifteen, girls until fourteen years of age. We have the minutes of the trustees for the boys' school from 1824, from which the following facts are gleaned. A five day school week was established in 1825—that is, if "vacated" for a half day because of mid-week meeting, then school to be held half of Seventh-day; if for a whole day because of Monthly Meeting, then all day Seventh-day. In the report to Monthly Meeting, 1825, it was estimated there were about 400 Quaker families in the city, and probably an equal number of children, one-half of whom, taught on a modern plan, at $1.00 per quarter, would incur no more expense on the Society than at present. There were then sixty pupils in the boys' school, three-fourths of whom were from the Northern District, for which the school was inconvenient. The monitorial system of teaching was proposed. Later that year the school property on Pearl Street was to be sold, and Goold Brown (member of meeting, and author of several grammars long used in schools) was to be paid $12.00 for rent for his school room (probably in Pearl Street) for a half month longer than had been agreed.

This same year $19.13 was paid for seven loads of wood. This high price for wood is perhaps the reason why we find Lehigh coal purchased in 1827. In 5th Month, 1826, Solomon Jenner engaged to teach the school on the most approved system of

QUAKERISM IN NEW YORK CITY 169

Monitorial instruction, for $1,000 per year, to begin as soon as the new school house in Elizabeth Street was ready.

The list of books to be used in this enlarged and modernized school is rather impressive, and quite an extension of the three Rs specified in 1788.

   Cobb's Spelling Book.
* N. Y. Expositor [by Samuel Wood].
   N. Y. Reader No. 1.
   New Testament.
* Murray's Reader and Sequel [by Lindley Murray].
* Day's Table Book [by Mahlon Day].
* Willett's Arithmetic and Geography [by Jacob Willetts].
   Woodbridge's Atlas.
* Brown's Grammar [by Goold Brown].
   Walker's Elocution.
   Clark's Catechism of Astronomy.
   Ryan's Astronomy and Algebra.
* Gummere's Surveying [by John Gummere].
   Bowditch's Navigation.
   Euclid's Geometry.
   Clark's Penmanship.

At least the six which I have starred were Quaker authors, and four of these were, at some period, members of the Monthly Meeting. As to the others, John Gummere (1784-1845) was a Pennsylvania Quaker, whose *Treatise on Surveying*, 1814, reached its fifteenth edition by 1854. His son, Samuel J. Gummere, was sometime principal of the Moses

Brown School, Providence, Rhode Island, and the latter's son, Francis B. Gummere, a professor at Haverford College. Jacob Willetts (1785-1860) was a Quaker teacher at Nine Partners and other schools. His *Easy Grammar of Geography,* 1814, passed through at least thirteen editions, and his *Scholar's Arithmetic,* 1816, reached its fourth edition in 1822.

The New Testament and Murray's Reader and Sequel were to be furnished by the trustees. The pupils appear to have been compelled to furnish the other books and to pay for the privilege of studying them. But corporal punishment was allowed only by permission of the Visiting Committee, and no pupil was to be discharged except by direction of the trustees. This school, as reestablished at Elizabeth Street, was a forward step in education, and probably was as good a school as could then be found in the New York which had just been joined with the Great Lakes by the Erie Canal; which would have a horse-drawn Harlem Railroad, and a $20,000,000 fire before a decade should pass; which had little water and no sewers; which had 2,500 grog shops, and an un-uniformed watch who carried lanterns on poles and cried the hours by night, and by day saw to it that the householders "shovel or sweep the refuse, garbage and ashes (for coal had been in use since 1820) to the middle of the street—where it fattened the pigs until it pleased the city officials to remove it." (Lanier's *A Century of Banking in New York, 1822-1922.*)

In 1826 the following rates were charged (stationary and fuel being extra).

1st	Class	Alphabet	$1.50	per quarter
2nd	"	Spelling	1.50	" "
3rd	"	Spelling, reading, writing and the tables of Arithmetic	2.50	" "
4th	"	Arithmetic through the simple rules, and Geography of U. S.	2.50	" "
5th	"	Arithmetic through compound rules, Geography of America and elements of English grammar	3.50	" "
6th	"	Arithmetic through the double rule of three, Geography of the world and English grammar through etymology	4.00	" "
7th	"	Arithmetic, English grammar, including composition and elocution, drawing of maps, History of Astronomy and the use of the globe	4.00	" "
8th	"	Book-Keeping, Surveying, Navigation, Geometry and Algebra	5.00	" "

The teacher requested that seven might sit at each desk instead of nine, and some of the seats attached to the desks were altered to allow this improvement.

In 5th Month, 1846, the Supply Committee reported having found a party who would buy the desks, and stated that the probable cost of seats with backs, and new desks, would not exceed $2.25 each. The trustees ordered them for both schools (boys' and girls'). In 8th Month a circular, prepared by the principals of the Male and Female departments, David J. Griscom and Cynthia S. Carpenter, was approved by the trustees, and 1,500 copies ordered of Mahlon Day.

This circular was headed with the new title—FRIENDS' INSTITUTE—and stated that the school was "entirely reorganized in every respect as the wants of the Monthly Meeting demand." New courses were to be added, including electro-magnetism and the steam engine. The school rooms were fitted with carpets, chairs, etc. The school year was to consist of two terms of twenty-two weeks each, the first beginning on the first Second day in 9th Month, and the second on the Second day following the close of the first term. Thus we find them giving up the Spartan simplicity of long backless benches and cumbersome desks for chairs and more modern apparatus; but still making of school attendance a serious business, with the first term extending without a break over Christmas and New Year's into February, and the second term beginning the *next week* and ending after the Fourth of July! But in place of the former boys' school and girls' school they were approaching co-education, and had become more definitely an institution of learning.

On removing to the present building in 1861, the name was changed to its present form—FRIENDS' SEMINARY—and the curriculum enlarged. The prospectus of that year stated that it would open on the 9th of 9th Month, with a school year of four quarters. The faculty for that year were Thomas Foulke, principal; Hugh Foulke, first teacher in the boys' department; Amanda K. Miller, first teacher in the girls' department; Mary Birdsall, teacher in the Primary department. French and other modern languages would be taught by competent native instructors. The fees were, per quarter: Primary, $7.00; Junior, $10.00; Junior Academic, $16.00; Senior Academic, $20.00. These fees included Latin in Junior and Senior grades. French was $5.00 additional, and German or other language $8.00 each. The fees for drawing and painting were to be "the professor's charges." In 1872, a slump having occurred in the fall enrolment, reasons for the discontinuance of fifty-eight pupils were ascertained, among them the following: too short a walk for one, too long for another, one objected to female teachers, another wished a Roman Catholic education, others had gone to higher schools, or to no school, to Europe, into business, etc. It is probable that the school was open to children of non-members from an early period. It was decided in 1846, that no child who was a member of the Society, and no child of a member, was to be excluded on account of inability to pay. The school appears to have been free to members of the Monthly Meeting from 1788.

In 1924 it became necessary to alter the building, and to improve on what had been best in 1861. In doing this room was found for one hundred additional pupils; the average attendance of 265 had theretofore crowded the capacity.

After the Separation of 1828 the Twentieth Street Friends (now so called) being without buildings, do not appear to have established a school until 1835, or at least the trustees then reported that they had hired a building nearly opposite the meeting house on Henry Street, and fitted it up for school purposes, under the care of David Sands as teacher. In 1842 a lot was purchased adjoining the north side of the Orchard Street meeting house, and a three story school house built on it. Here a Monthly Meeting school was held until 1859. In 1850 there were thirteen boys and fifteen girls in the school. I have not learned anything later of this school. Perhaps the development of Friends' Seminary was thought to fill the need thereafter, and their children went there.

Friends' Seminary has had a worthy past. What it may be in the next half century, in the larger city, none can say, but we may be sure that the need for it will be no less.

A word regarding Joseph Lancaster (1778-1839) appears appropriate, as his educational system, the Monitorial or Lancasterian, was used from the beginning in the schools of the Public School Society and for several years in Friends' Seminary. He joined the Society of Friends in England in 1794 and was disowned in 1814 for financial carelessness. He saw the need for a more rapid spread of education, and opened a school in 1796 which by 1801 had a thousand pupils, the more advanced ones acting as monitors to train the younger ones. By 1811 he had established 95 schools attended by 30,000 children. He came to America in 1818 and received high honors. He died in New York from a carriage accident; was buried in the Houston Street burial ground, and in 1874 his remains were transferred to Greenwood Cemetery.

The libraries maintained by the Society may be considered as an educational matter. There are two at Twentieth Street and two at Fifteenth Street. There are also libraries at the Brooklyn Meeting houses. Some of these books were by the authors, or printed by the Quaker printers, elsewhere mentioned. Together they form a collection valuable for the student. Several volumes remain from what was once "Penn's Library at Friends' Institute," but I have learned nothing further of that library.

The Public School System

New York Friends were concerned for proper education not alone of Quaker children, but for the increasing number in the city who must perforce grow up without even the three Rs. In many reforms furthered by our Society, the minutes of the meeting show no clue until after the first stage of progress. This is especially true in relation to the establishment of the Public School system. In *In the Olden Time*, by Sarah S. Murray, 1894, p. 106 *et seq.* and in other books, is related how the "Association for the Relief of the Sick Poor," held its first meeting at the house of John Murray, Jr., 3d Month 21, 1798. John Murray, Jr., had married Catharine Bowne (a descendant of John Bowne, of Flushing) in 1783. Catharine Murray was appointed treasurer of the Association, and held that office for nineteen years. In 5th Month, 1800, they rented a room and engaged a "widowwoman," Theresa Gavan, of good education and morals, at £30 per annum, she to furnish the firewood. They were incorporated in 1813, and by 1817 there were six hundred girls in the several schools of the "Female Association" as it had early become known. *The New York Public School*, by A. E. Palmer, 1905, which is an excellent history of the development of public education in this city, states that the Female Association had about seven hundred and fifty pupils in 1825 when their schools were excluded from assistance by public money, for the reason that they were chiefly under the patronage of members of the Society of Friends. They continued until 1845, when they were absorbed into the Public School Society. The ladies who organized the Association and were its earliest members were all Quakers. Their names are worthy of record:

Catharine Murray	Hannah Pearsall
Elizabeth Bowne	Margaret B. Haydock
Sarah Robinson	Sarah Haydock
Amy Bowne	Mary Pearsall Robinson
Amy Clark	Amy Underhill
Elizabeth U. Underhill	Caroline Bowne
Martha Stansbury	Hannah Shelton
Jane Johnston	E. Huyland Walker
Susan Collins	Sarah Hallet
Elizabeth Burling	Sarah Bowne Minturn
Harriet Robbins	Mary Minturn, Jr.
Sarah Tallman	Deborah Minturn Watt
Hannah Eddy	Hannah Bowne
Ann Eddy	Ann Shipley
Agnes A. Watt	Hannah Lawrence
Sarah Collins	M. Minturn
Elizabeth Pearsall	Esther Robinson Minturn
Mary R. Bowne	Mary Dunbar
Rebecca Haydock	Mary Wright
Penelope Hull	Sarah Lyons Kirby
Mary Murray	Charlotte Perkins

In James Grant Wilson's excellent *Memorial History of New York,* 1893, III, 164-168, is given a good account of the beginnings of public education in this city. "An association of ladies belonging to the Society of Friends, or Quakers, had contributed of their private means and established a free school for the education of girls. This humble but noble endeavor was the germ of the great metropolitan system of public schools of to-day." The *Life of Thomas Eddy,* by Samuel L. Knapp, 1834, states that New York State was behind the New England states in education, not yet rising to the ideal of taxing all for the benefit of all. John Murray, Jr., and Thomas Franklin proposed an association of Quakers to establish a free school for poor children not of our Society, but Thomas Eddy objected that it would be impossible to do so except on a small scale, and proposed calling to their aid respectable citizens of different denominations. A meeting was therefore called on February 19, 1805, at John Murray's house on Pearl Street. Besides these three, Thomas Pearsall, also a member of meeting, and eight non-members were gathered in conference. These latter were Samuel Osgood, Brockholst Livingston, Samuel Miller, Joseph Constant, Matthew Clarkson, Leonard Bleecker, Samuel Russell and William Edgar. Samuel Osgood (1748-1813) graduated from Harvard in 1770, served honorably in several capacities through the Revolutionary War, was repeatedly a member of the legislature of Massachusetts, was the first Commissioner of the United States Treasury, and was the first Postmaster General. When the Government removed in 1791 to Philadelphia he remained in New York, residing on Franklin Square, and served in the State Senate. For the last ten years of his life he was U. S. Naval Officer at this port. He also found time to be a merchant. He was well versed in science and literature, and published several volumes on religious subjects and one on chronology. Brockholst Livingston, LL.D. (1757-1823) was a Judge of the Supreme Court of the State, and became in 1806 a judge of the Supreme Court of the United States. Samuel Miller, D.D. (1770-1850) was then pastor of the Brick Church, later professor of Ecclesiastical History in Princeton Theological Seminary, and always earnest in the cause of education. Matthew Clarkson (1759-1825) had been a general in the American Revolution, distinguished for his courage, talents and integrity, and was in later years an active member and Vice President of the American Bible Society. I have not learned details of the four others, but as Eddy and Murray had selected them I am sure they were forward looking representative men of the city and probably noted in their day, if now forgotten. Of John Murray, Jr., it is said that when offered a partnership in the firm of Murray, Sanson and Company by his father, he declined it from a sense of religious duty, feeling that he had acquired a competent share of this world's goods, and soon thereafter retired from commerce. He was active in the Manumission Society from its establishment in 1786, in work for the welfare of the Indians from 1795, and in Penal Reform from 1796, till his death. The remarkable character of Thomas Eddy is considered under the heading of "Quakers in Civil and Public Life."

As a result of this important discussion in the pleasant candle-lit parlor on Pearl Street, "The Society for establishing a Free School in the City of New York for the education of such poor children as do not belong to, or are not provided for, by any religious Society," was incorporated April 9, 1806, with De Witt Clinton (then Mayor) and the twelve above named, as the first board of trustees. They established School No. 1 that year, on Chatham Street, according to James Grant Wilson, and had twelve pupils at the start. *The Public Schools of New York*, in the *Tribune Monthly*, March, 1896, states that Grammar School No. 1 is the successor to Public School No. 1, established in 1806, in the basement of a tenement house in Bancker (now Madison) Street, with 42 scholars. The first building for this school, 50 x 150 feet, was used until 1856, when the school was removed to William Street near Duane. A view of this original building is shown. I will not try to reconcile these conflicting accounts, but am inclined to accept the lesser number of pupils; the tenement house did not reach New York until thirty years later. The name of the organization was soon changed to the "Public School Society." At first confined to the poor, its benefits were gradually extended to all classes. The *History of the Public School Society*, by William O. Bourne, 1870, shows how its work was taken over in 1853 by the Board of Education, and its schools No. 1 to 18 (as then numbered) transferred to the Board, which had been established in 1842 and had already built some schools of its own. The schools of the Manumission Society, for colored children, had been taken over by the Public School Society in 1834, with about 1,400 registered pupils. The Society had long had financial assistance with public money. "Nowhere else [than in N. Y.] were the Schools and the school moneys, during a long course of years, placed under the control of a private corporation, having no direct responsibility to the people." (*N. Y. Public Schools*, p. 198.) I think that Public School No. 1 might properly bear the name "Catharine Bowne Murray School" in memory of its origin. Quakers were always prominent in the Public School Society, and the following named Friends were connected with it, in addition to those above mentioned:

Lindley Murray *	John L. Bowne
Samuel F. Mott	W. H. Barrow
Joseph B. Collins	Isaac Collins

* See footnote on page 182.

Barney Corse
Mahlon Day
James S. Gibbons
George T. Trimble *
Joshua S. Underhill
William Burling
Thomas Bussing
Benjamin S. Collins
Isaac H. Clapp
Samuel Hicks
Anthony P. Halsey
Edmund Kirby
William H. Macy
James B. Nelson
Jeremiah Thompson
Samuel Wood
William Seaman
Joshua Underhill
William Willis
Benjamin Clark
Whitehead Hicks
George F. Hussey
Benjamin Minturn

George Newbold
W. T. Slocum
James W. Underhill
Robert W. Cornell
Willett Seaman
Walter Underhill
Thomas Buckley
Walter Bowne
William Birdsall
Nathan Comstock
Richard Cromwell
William P. Cooledge
Matthew Franklin
Valentine Hicks
Henry Hinsdale
T. Leggett, Jr.
Robert F. Mott
Samuel C. Mott
Benjamin D. Perkins
William R. Thurston, Jr.
Edmund Willets
David Sands
Ira S. Underhill

Of these, Lindley Murray served 29 years, Joseph B. Collins, Benjamin Clark and Robert W. Cornell each 25 years, Mahlon Day 24 years, Samuel F. Mott and Samuel Wood each 20 years, and George

* For good portraits of George T. Trimble, and of Lindley Murray, see the *History of the Public School Society,* pp. 320 and 480.

T. Trimble 36 years, he being the last President. De Witt Clinton, who as Mayor, was properly made one of the first board of trustees, had married, in 1796, Matthew Franklin's daughter Maria.

Efforts of New York Friends in the education of Negroes are considered under "Negroes and Slavery."

The Flushing Female Association, which was organized in 1814, and did a work similar to that in New York, was composed chiefly of Quakers. (*History of Flushing*, Waller, p. 175.)

The Monthly Meeting: Its Habitat; Its Business Methods

The Quarterly Meeting decided in 6th Month (August) 1672, that "ffriends of ye monthly meeting of New Yorke and Gravesend doe agree yt ye monthly meeting is to be kept at Yorke two month following & ye 3d at Graves end and the first Meeting att Graves end to be ye first fourth day in the 6th mo & soe sucksesifly." On the 20th of 3d Month (May) 1684, the Quarterly Meeting determined further, "Then agreed by friends at this meeting yt ffriends at Yorke Gravesend and Flushing & Westchester ye kills and Newtown doe all belonge unto one Monthly meeting & soe to remain, at Gravesend at ye 4th quarterly meeting & soe to continue by their own appointing wt place they see convenient after." By 1695 it was meeting solely at Flushing, and so met until 8th Month (October) 1742, then at Flushing and Newtown till 6th Month (June) 1768, then at Flushing, Newtown and New York in rotation until 11th Month, 1780, after which, twice at New York, and once at Flushing. It changed its name to the "Monthly Meeting of Friends of New York," 7th Month 1, 1795. Flushing was set off as a separate Monthly Meeting 6th Month 5, 1805, with the

Preparative Meeting of Flushing and the old Newtown meeting for worship at Maspeth Kills. The Monthly Meeting was first held at Liberty Street, then at Pearl Street, then at Hester Street, but the dates of removal are not exactly known. From Hester Street the "liberal" branch removed to Fifteenth Street in 1861. Joint sessions of men and women were adopted 4th Month 5, 1902. It has been held alternately in New York and Brooklyn since 2d Month 7, 1903. Newark Monthly Meeting was established 12th Month 2, 1917, being set off from this Monthly Meeting. What is now called Twentieth Street Monthly Meeting was held at Henry Street until 1840, then at Orchard Street till 1857, since which time at Twentieth Street.

A word as to the method in Quaker business meetings. Any matter may be brought before the meeting at any session, by any member of that meeting. If a sufficient degree of unity therewith appears, the Clerk writes and offers a minute embodying the matter. If the approval appears general, opposers generally withdraw their objections, or silently acquiesce, and the Clerk states that the subject appears to be approved. If a large proportion of the members express disapproval, or if a few continue opposition, the Clerk usually states that way does not appear to open, or that there is not sufficient unity of expression, to proceed. It is decision by unanimous consent, and while subject to the abuse of delay by stubborn objection of one or two members of influence, is, on the whole an excellent method of decision and productive of fewer heartburnings than do decisions by a majority of one. An equally important matter is the reading of each minute as it is agreed upon. Other organizations are to-day adopting the practise of reading and approving the minutes of the meeting before its adjournment, to avoid the risk of erroneous minutes causing inconvenience or trouble by not being corrected until the next meeting.

The Monthly Meeting is the executive body of the Quaker organization, the Yearly Meeting being the legislative body. Membership and the administration of discipline pertain to the Monthly Meeting.

The Preparative Meetings

The Preparative Meeting was for many years of the nature of a select committee. It was not until 6th Month 9, 1753, that "it is Concluded at this meeting that Each weeke meeting have a preparative meeting within themselves on the Days proposed," and further, "it is ye mind of the meeting that all ffriends that are Esteemed proper members of ye monthly meet shaul be of ye prepareative meeting."

The original Preparative Meeting of New York (of which we have records only from 1781) was doubtless first held at Liberty Street, but had apparently been held at Pearl Street for several years, when, beginning 1st Month 29, 1807, it was called "for the Eastern District" (because another Preparative Meeting was then established), and was held at Pearl Street until 1824, then (by Fifteenth Street Friends) at Rose Street until 1856, then at Hester Street until 4th Month, 1861, since which time at Fifteenth Street. Joint sessions were adopted in 1902.

A division of the growing meeting was made, and a Preparative Meeting for the Western District was established 12th Month 31, 1806, and held at Liberty Street until 11th Month 28, 1822, when it was laid down and the members attached to the Eastern District at Pearl Street. It appears probable that the original Preparative Meeting was removed to Pearl

Street to suit the convenience of the greater number of members, and that later another was set up at Liberty Street and maintained there until shortly before that house was abandoned.

A Preparative Meeting for the Northern District was established in 1820 in the new meeting house on Hester Street. This was laid down 5th Month 22, 1856, on which date the original Preparative Meeting, held at Rose Street for several years, was removed to Hester Street, and absorbed the members of this meeting.

A Preparative Meeting for the Western District (the second so called) was established in 1832 on Downing Street "at Greenwich." The name was changed 5th Month 21, 1856, to Northern District, and it was removed 12th Month, 1856, to Twenty-seventh Street, where it remained until 6th Month 30, 1881, when it was laid down, and the members attached to Fifteenth Street Preparative Meeting, which has since been called "Preparative Meeting for Friends of New York."

A Preparative Meeting was set up at Henry Street in 1828 by the Twentieth Street branch, to which all Friends of their side were attached. It was removed with the meeting houses, and is now held at Twentieth Street. Joint sessions were adopted in 1880.

The Brooklyn Preparative Meetings of both branches have been sufficiently noticed in connection with their meeting houses.

The Records

The records of the Monthly Meeting, its subordinate meetings and subsidiary organizations, are numerous and valuable. They give an intimate picture of the social life, and somewhat of the special contribution of the Quakers to the religious life of this city, to those who can read the crabbed lines of some clerks, the beautiful penmanship of others, and between the lines of all clerks, and who can feel, behind the chirography the spirit which produced the minutes. There are noble and inspiring sentiments; there are items that sadden us by showing our ancestors to have been no better than ourselves; there are entries written in deep seriousness, which to unaccustomed eyes appear richly humorous.

The earliest dated Quaker records in this colony are marriage certificates beginning with 1663, in a vellum bound book into which they were copied in 1685 "from ye originall" by Isaac Horner, and preceded by an account of the famous case at Nottingham assizes in 1661, when the judge decided, as a matter of law, that it was the consent of the parties that made a marriage, thereby certifying the legality of the simple Quaker form of marriage ceremony. The earliest book of records is one which, unbound or in a paper cover, George Fox sent here by the hand of John Burnyeat, containing Fox's Papers of Advice. These had been sent in 1669 and 1670 to every Monthly Meeting in England, and are the basis of every book of Discipline which Quakers have anywhere produced. Burnyeat was at the Half-Yearly Meeting at Oyster Bay, the 23rd of 3rd Month (May) 1671, and at that Meeting the earliest minute in America was written in the book he had brought, as follows: "at a mens meet ye 23^d day of 3^d month: 1671. It was agreed yt ye first dayes meetings be one day at oysterbay and another day at Matinacock: to begin at or about the first houre: in ye afternoone It [was] all So ageeded [agreed] ther Shall bee a meetting keept at the wood edege [Westbury] the 25th of the 4th month and Soe ever[y] 5th first Day of the weeke." From that date to the present there are fairly continuous records, the Monthly Meeting being regularly held since 1682. This book, containing the earliest minute, and used for Monthly, Quarterly and Yearly Meeting minutes (the latter established 1696) until 1703, lay forgotten in the garret of the Bowne house at Flushing until about sixty years ago.

The following extract from the minutes shows that care was sometimes taken for their preservation. The matter being proposed 12th Month, 1772, a committee was appointed the following month "to Collect the minutes of this monthly Meeting as far back as may be and report their Service." In 5th

Earliest Quaker Minute in America

Month, 1773, the committee reported "that what they have yet found begins with 4 mo. 1742 and that from thence to this time there is several Omissions Vz 5 mo. 1742, 11 & 12 mo. 1751, 1 mo. 1752, 4 mo. 1760, 9th 10th 11th & 12th mo. 1769, all the months in 1770, & 1st mo. 1771." They were desired to continue their care "to enquire Occasionally and report when they make further discovereyes." Interest appears to have subsided, for the minutes for 2d, 3d, 4th and 5th Months, 1771, are also missing. I have found no later report of this committee, nor do I know when or where the minutes previous to 1742 were found, but they were well preserved, unbound, and have since been bound. The "Book of Records," a parchment bound volume, contains a complete copy, in the minute and exact hand of Isaac Horner, of the Papers of Advice of George Fox. This was mislaid for a century and a half, and recently sent in.

Certificates of removal were not recorded in the minutes after 1722 (and only certain important ones previously) until 1778, since which a complete record has been kept. Of the certificates received in the interval, many originals have been preserved, and are now mounted in books. Registration of vital data, births from 1640, deaths from 1669, have been fairly well kept, escaping the neglect which occurred in many Monthly Meetings late in the eighteenth century. Yet several individuals whose names are not in these records, showed in their wills or deeds that they were Quakers. In 1800, in connection with the publication of the revised and first printed Discipline, a renewed interest in the vital records began. This again flagged in some meetings, but since 1810, when the Discipline was again revised, vital records have been kept with care. Burial records for this Monthly Meeting have been kept since 1798. The minutes of the Ministers and Elders are complete from 1759. The book in which these were recorded was also used for the Yearly Meeting of Ministers and Elders, beginning 1704, for 188 years. The Treasurer's record from 1784 to 1809 and from 1828 to the present time, are preserved. There are also the minutes of the Preparative Meetings, and of the numerous standing committees and subsidiary organizations. One result of the unfortunate Separation is the double sets of books thereafter, for what are now Fifteenth and Twentieth Street meetings.

All of these records are included in the collection of nearly seventeen hundred volumes cared for by the Joint Committee on Records, and preserved in fireproof safes in the Record Room at Friends Seminary, 15 Rutherford Place, New York. There are also many first editions and rare books by Quaker authors, in the Record Room.

Cemeteries

The first Quaker cemetery in this city was behind the meeting house on what is now Liberty Place. This was later enlarged by the purchase of the second meeting house plot, fronting on Liberty Street. A law of 1823 prohibited burials below Grand Street. When the Liberty Street house and ground was sold in 1825 the remains were removed to a vault in the new cemetery which had been purchased in 1796, on the south side of East Houston (formerly North) Street, near Christie (formerly First) Street. St. Augustine's Episcopalian Church now occupies the greater part of this land. This cemetery was extended in 1817 by the purchase of land adjoining it on the south, fronting on Christie Street. Remains from the Pearl Street burial ground were also removed to this cemetery. No burials were made here after the present cemetery in Prospect Park was opened, in 1846. Some remains were removed thereafter to the latter cemetery, and in 1874 the Houston Street ground was sold. The minutes of Fifteenth Street Monthly Meeting for 4th Month, 1874, include a report of the Property Committee which stated that "In the year 1826 (nearly 50 years ago) the remains of those who had been interred in Friends' burial ground in

Liberty Street, this city, were removed and deposited in a brick vault, built for that purpose in the Houston Street Ground. These remains are being again removed and placed in the ground at Westbury; where we trust they will be permitted to remain without danger of further disturbance." The expense of this removal, to the Friends' burial ground at Westbury was borne two-thirds by Fifteenth Street meeting and one-third by Twentieth Street meeting. The Houston Street property was sold, and the proceeds divided between the meetings in the same proportions.

In 1846 nine acres were purchased on the Coney Island Plank Road outside of Brooklyn, for a cemetery, after which some individuals removed remains from Houston Street thither. The reason that the wholesale removal of 1874 was to Westbury was probably owing to the opening of Prospect Park in 1871, and the possibility that the cemetery might later be taken for park purposes. The park now entirely surrounds and hides the cemetery, the entrance to which, near a park gate, is inconspicuously situated. Under date of 11th Month, 1850, the Meeting minutes show that in 1824 the Town Meeting of Brooklyn had established a cemetery, which was confirmed by the Legislature in 1828. Of this a portion was later allotted to the Quakers. Burials were prohibited in 1850, and a street was to be cut through, whereupon the meeting removed its dead to the cemetery now in Prospect Park, and sold the land.

Gravestones began to appear by 1762, or at least then to trouble the Meeting. Committee after committee was appointed during the next decade to "remove superfluous stones." At Flushing and New York all were soon removed, except some which were nearly level with the ground, but some were reset by non-members, and the committee was directed to remove one and all. The weekly meeting in Newtown was desired to have the gravestones removed from its burial ground. The neat and wholly desirable custom of keeping the sod level, without mound or flower bed, as in English Quaker burial grounds, and in the beautiful Arlington cemetery at Washington, has not yet been adopted in this cemetery, but it is to be hoped that this simple reform may be brought about, it being no more logical to have a mound kept up over the mortal part of a loved one than to wear for a time, or forever, a black band on the arm.

Simplicity and avoidance of ostentation at funerals and in the care of the burial place must appeal to the sober good sense of many people. But in the grief of bereavement a desire to show honor to the memory of the deceased, intensified by a consideration of what others may say or think, frequently outweighs this sober good sense. It is probable that in a majority of cases the cost of funeral and tombstone is beyond propriety, and that where it is the wage earner or the mother of the home who has gone it is a doubly serious burden on the living, and of no avail to the dead. The ostentatious monuments in fashionable cemeteries are a sad sight to the reflective mind. A stroll through the pleasant cemetery in Prospect Park brings no sadness. Here is Peace and Rest. Here is no distinction between the millionaire and the member who received assistance from the Meeting, whose bodies must alike return to the good mother earth.

The Separation of 1828

In the year 1828 the Society of Friends split into two parties, here as in most of the meetings in America. There is a plethora of published matter available on the fact and its causes, by participants and partisans. The reader is welcome to study that and form conclusions. I will only attempt to show the color-blindness of both parties to the "Light which lighteth every man." The Separation was not alone the greatest misfortune of American Quakerism—it was a tragedy. The Society of Friends became two societies of enemies. The pros and cons of the controversy which raged throughout most of American Quakerdom have been discussed many times, generally in a partisan spirit. They are, in legal parlance, irrelevant and immaterial to this study of history. What has not sufficiently been set forth by partisan writers is that the separation could not have occurred had Friends been earnestly awake to the Inward Light as George Fox expressed it. Narrowness of mind and poverty of soul can alone account for the bitter feud. And, as shown in another chapter, this happened in the golden age of worldly prosperity for members of this meeting. Hervey Allen, in *Israfel* (p. 673) summarizes the religious conditions of

America in the first half of the nineteenth century, "Puritanism, Quakerism and Calvinism all alike were in process of disintegration."

The vibrant faith and burning zeal of the First Publishers had been long forgotten; the trials endured, the temptations resisted by the early Friends, —imprisonment, banishment, fines, distraints—all of which might have been avoided by compromise and evasion; these too were forgotten. The early simplicity of dress had developed into a uniform, variation from which was frowned upon and punished by disownment. The democracy of thought originally expressed in retaining the use of the unfashionable singular pronoun had become a badge of membership, lapses into the vernacular being discouraged equally with the sartorial offenses. The divine common sense of Fox, expressed in his "papers of advice"—a fluid testimony—had been solidified into a rigid system of conduct. The nature of Quakerism tends to the development of strong individuality, and this very strength of individuality, under these artificial conditions, made possible that pitiable quarrel. The few who actually caused the split—and they were few—were, on each side, not only sure that they were Right, but equally sure that the others were Wrong. Instead of intelligent and consecrated leadership there was bossism; the effect was centrifugal rather than centripetal. Differences of belief, of mental attitude, had arisen; they have since become more marked;

but in the five branches into which Quakerism in America is now divided there appears to be no broader range of belief or thought than is found in English Quakerdom, which, under wiser leadership, has remained undivided. The Separation appears to have been as inevitably an effect of these causes as was the French Revolution a result of the evils which preceded it.

At this unfortunate time those who now are called Twentieth Street Friends, being somewhat in the minority, left the session of the Yearly Meeting, and held Yearly Meeting elsewhere. The same process occurred in the Monthly Meeting, and would in itself have given a pretense of ownership to the Fifteenth Street Friends. But added to that was the fact that the trustees of the property were all, or nearly all, of the latter side. The result was that all the meeting houses in the city were thereafter in legal possession of the Fifteenth Street Friends. That the bitterness of that sad time did not lead to later injustice is shown by the fact that a committee of the latter body was soon appointed to deed certain real estate (not the meeting houses) to the other body, and that when in 1846 the cemetery in Prospect Park was purchased, the Twentieth Street Friends purchased a parcel adjoining, and wished to buy a portion of the land purchased by Fifteenth Street Friends, whereupon the latter made a deed of gift to them for the land they needed. So our dead have lain peacefully together for eighty years, separated only by a driveway, and cared for by a joint employee of the two bodies. Likewise in 1874, the proceeds of the sale of the Houston Street cemetery, and the cost of removal to Westbury, were amicably divided.

Latterly several of the Twentieth Street children have been educated at the one Quaker school at Sixteenth Street; their young people have long met socially; there have been intermarriages; the Young Friends' Movement has opened the eyes of all to each other's virtues, and their hearts more fully to the Eternal Love, common alike to them and to all who earnestly desire it. Many older Friends on both sides have become younger in mind and heart through the fellowship of the Joint Committee on Affiliated Service, so that at present it appears that habit alone separates the severed branches. Habit, of thought, of action, of old ways, is a powerful force of inertia, but forward-looking souls—pioneer spirits—can and do break its thrall. All of this is borne out in the joint sessions of the two Yearly Meetings of 1924, in commemoration of the tercentenary of the birth of George Fox; in the Yearly Meeting of 1928, held jointly in penitent commemoration of the Separation; in the close fellowship and fraternity of metropolitan Friends. Organic union is not proposed, but an increasing cooperation of effort and unity of spirit are everywhere evident, as in the All American Friends' Conference, at Oskaloosa, Iowa, in 1929.

"The Conclusion of the Whole Matter"

Although I have not herein dwelt lengthily on the meeting for worship, the highest expression of our corporate life, and will leave a larger treatment of that for some better fitted mentality and spirit, I have tried to show how Quakerism, planted in faith, watered with tears of suffering, enriched by blood of cruel persecution, here sprang up and waxed strong. How, as the organization attained numerical strength, and the members acquired wealth, and as all vestiges of persecution disappeared, the meeting lost in spirituality while more and more codifying the Discipline. Which was cause and which effect it is not now essential to determine. The net result was a condition which allowed the Society to split into rival factions, each claiming to be the true body. One of these branches generally disowned every member of the other branch; the other, while priding itself on not disowning wholesale, did however disown such a member, and under such conditions, that we now see there was on each side such narrowness of mind, such weakened spirituality, that the wonder is not that the Society greatly decreased but rather that anything was left of it.

The renaissance appears to have begun with the

First-day School movement among Fifteenth Street Friends and the Bible School among those of Twentieth Street; it became more manifest in the Young Friends' Association; it is now evidenced in the Young Friends' Movement, the American Friends' Service, all the many joint activities of the two "Streets." It promises hopefully for a brighter, better future, in which the Meeting and its members may become ever more useful and helpful to this city and to the world. The joint Yearly Meeting of 1928 was a centennial commemoration of the deplorable Separation, penitential and pentecostal.

The expansion of the nation after the end of the Colonial period, 1783, brought opportunities which the Quakers failed to fully use. They now appear to have possibilities for the service of God and Mankind such as never before has been their lot. Their Service in Europe has brought them to the pleasant but dangerous condition of which Jesus warned his disciples—"Beware when all men speak well of you."

If I have not clearly shown the ways and methods, the deep earnestness and faithful efforts toward godliness, the breadth of philanthropy and kindliness of charity of the Friends—or if on the other hand I have seemed to overstress them—I count it my misfortune, but plead it to be no intentional partisanship. I have purposely avoided identifying many individuals herein mentioned as to the meeting to which each belonged, believing that "by one spirit are we all baptized into one body . . . for the body is not one but many." (*I Corinthians XII, 13.*) It is my hope and faith that we shall more and more join the work of our hands and the sympathies of our hearts, until all shall come to know, as an everlasting certainty, that nothing can separate us from one another, as "nothing shall separate us from the love of God."

Appendix

The following is the text of a Quaker marriage certificate of 1698. Since then the wording and spelling have somewhat changed, but not the intent and meaning.

Whereas there hath bine Intentions of Marridge betwene James Cock son of James Cock and Hana ffeake daughter of John & Elizabeth ffeake all of Motinicocke in the bounds of Oysterbay one Longisland in thy province of new yorke these are to certifie the truth to all people that it may concerne that James Cocke and Hana ffeake haveing laid theire intentions before two severall meettings of our men and Women called Quakers and persons having been Appointed by the said meetting to make Dilligent enquirey of Theire Clearness from all others in relation to Maridge and at thire second coming before our meeting all things being found Cleare and with consent of parents and Relations the said meetting freely consented to thire proseeding; and at the house of John feakes at motenicong in the bounds of Oysterbay the first day of ye tenth month 1698 at a meeting of the people called Quakers apointed for that pourpose the partis aforesaid James Cocke and Hana ffeake Did Stand up and solemnly declare that in the presents of god and his people they tooke Each other husband and wife promiseing to Each other to live together in love ffaithfullness till Death shall seperate us and for further Confermation they have seet thier hands ye day and year above Written in the presents of us whose names are under Written being Wittnesses thereunto

Edward Whitex	Mary Pryor	James Cock
William ffry	William Willis	Hannah Cock
John Cock	Daniel Underhill	John ffek
Thomas Willetts	Samuel Underhill	Elizabeth feke
Thomas Willits	John Evens	Sarah Cock
Tho: Chalkley	Samuel titus	Mary bowne
Richard Willits	Samuel macoun	Elizabeth Bradford
Joseph Thorn	beniamen Carpenter	Mary Willis
Samuel Bowne		Elisebeth Smith
Robert ffield	Henry Cock	Hannah Titus
	Robert Feek	Joseph Smith
	Mary Feek	
	Elizabeth ffeeke	

Thomas Chalkley, the noted minister, who signed as a witness, says of his visit, "We had a meeting at a place called *Matinicock,* where I met with some of the people called *Ranters,* who disturbed our meeting. I may say as the apostle *Paul* (only altering *Ephesus* to *Matinecock,*) I fought with beasts there." Another witness was Elizabeth (Sowle) Bradford, wife of William, the Printer.

The following is the text of the first deed for land for a Quaker Meeting-house on Manhattan Island. It is on parchment, and engrossed in a blackletter style. The original is 24 x 11½ inches plus the fold at bottom. The red seals show a shield with crest and supporters. In lower half a chevron enclosing some small object. In upper half several small objects. All in excellent condition.

THIS INDENTURE made the fifth day of August ANNO DNI 1696 And in the Eighth yeare of the Reigne of William the Third King of England Scotland ffrance and Ireland Defender of the ffaith &c BETWEEN David Lloyd of the City of Philadelphia in the Provence of Pensylvania Gentleman and Isaac Norris of the said City Merchant Executors of the last Will and Testament of Thomas Lloyd of the said City Gentleman deceased of the one part and William Bickley of the City of New York Merchant John Rodman of fflushing on the Island of Nassau Physician and Thomas Stevens and Edward Stevens of New Towne on the Island aforesaid Yeomen on the other part WITTNESSETH That the said David Lloyd and Isaac Norris for and in Consideration of the sume of Twenty five pounds Currant money of New York aforesaid by them in hand at and before the ensealeing of these p^{r}sents well and truly paid the Receipt whereof the said David Lloyd and Isaac Norris doe hereby Acknowledge and thereof and of every part and parcell thereof doe hereby Acquitt Release and Discharge them the said William Bickley John Rodman Thomas Stevens and Edward Stevens and every of them theire and every of theire heires Executors and Admstrators HAVE Granted Bargained Sold Enfeoffed Conveyed and Confirmed And by these p^{r}sents Doe Grant Bargaine Sell Enfeoffe Convey and Confirme unto them the said William Bickley John Rodman Thomas Stevens and Edward Stevens & theire heires for ever ALL THAT a Certeine parcell of Land Scituate Lying and being in the City of New York aforesaid fronting Easterly to a Certeine Street newly layd out called Greene Street bounded South by the Land of the said John Rodman Westerly by the Land of Edward Burling and Northerly by some vacant Lotts Conteyning in Breadth ffront and Reare each end fforty foot and in Length on parrallell Lines Eighty foot English Measure. And all the Estate Right Title Interest property possession Reverson and Reversons Remainder and Remainders Dowers Titles of Dower Claime and Demand whatsoever of them the said David Lloyd and Isaac Norris of in or to the p^{r}misses or any part or parcell thereof TO HAVE AND TO HOLD the said parcell of Land and p^{r}misses herein before menconed to be Granted Sold and Conveyed with all and singuler the Appurtences unto them the said William Bickley John Rodman Thomas Stevens and Edward Stevens theire heires and Assignes To the only proper use Beneffitt and Behoofe of them the said William Bickley John Rodman Thomas Stevens and Edward Stevens theire heires and Assignes for ever AND THE SAID David Lloyd and Isaac Norris for themselves theire heires Executors and Admstrators doe Covenant promise and Grant to and with the said William Bickley John Rodman Thomas Stevens and Edward Stevens theire heires and Assignes and every of the   at they the said William Bickley John Rodman Thomas Stevens and Edward Stevens theire heires and Assignes shall and may peaceably and Quietly have hold use and Enjoy all the said before Granted p^{r}misses according to the true Intent and meaneing hereof And that the said David Lloyd and Isaac Norris theire heires and Assignes and all other person and persons Claimeing any Estate or Title to the p^rmisses before Granted shall and will for and dureing the space of Seven yeares next ensueing at the Reasonable Request Costs and Charges of them the said William Bickley John Rodman Thomas Stevens and Edward Stevens theire heires or Assignes Doe make Acknowledge Execute and Suffer or cause and procure to be done made Acknowledged Executed and Suffered all and every such further and other Act and Acts Lawfull and Reasonable Assureance and Assureances in the Law whatsoever for the further and better Conveying and Assureing of the p^rmisses before Granted unto them the said William Bickley John Rodman Thomas Stevens and Edward Stevens theire heires and Assignes according to the true Intent and meaneing hereof as by the said William Bickley John Rodman Thomas Stevens and Edward Stevens theire heires or Assignes or theire Councill learned in the Law shall be Devised Advised or Required IN WITTNESSE whereof the said David Lloyd and Isaac Norris have to this p^rsent Indenture sett theire hands and Seales the day and yeare first above written

  Da^d [Seal] Lloyd   Isaac [Seal] Norris

On the back of the deed is the following:

  Sealed and delivered
  in the p^rsence of vs
     James Mills
No 6   Wm Huddleston

Memorand That on the 10th day of December Anoq Dni 1698

Then Appeared before me John Guest Esq[r] one of his Majtys Justices of the Supream Court for the Province of New York William Huddleston one of the Wittness to the within Written Instrument and declared upon the Holy Evangelyst that he saw David Lloyd and Isaac Norris within menconed signe seale and deliver this within Written Indenture of Conveyance as their and each of their Voluntary act and Deed. John Guest.

Recorded in y[e] Office of Town Clerk of y[e] Citty of New Yorke in lib N° 23 page 34 Comp & Examd. & Will Harpas C[l]

Dav[d] loyd & Isaac Norris for a Lott of Ground in New York to W[m] bickley jn° Rodman Thomas & Edward Stevenson, for to buld a meeting house at York

Index

Besides the usual abbreviations the following are used:

ack. for acknowledged
estab. for established
F. A. for Female Association
Frds. for Friends
m. cert. for marriage certificate
m. out for married out
ment. for mentioned
M. M. for Monthly Meeting

N. A. for New Amsterdam
P. M. for Preparative Meeting
Pub. Sch. Soc. for Public School Society
Q. for Quaker or Quakers
Wms. for women's
Y. M. for Yearly Meeting

Abolitionist, I. T. Hopper, 79
Academy, Goold Brown's, 123
Academy of medicine, Valentine Mott, Pres., 151; Chas. MacDowell, Pres., 158; ment., 157
A Century of Banking, 170
Acknowledgment, to be made public as the offense, 84, 89
Adams, John, aided by Meeting to pay for slave, 42, 55
Address to Colonial Governor, 72; to Legislature *re* permitting slave trading vessels to fit out from N. Y., 60
Adult School, the, 52
Africa, fitting out of slave-trade vessels for, 61
African Free Schools, history of, 61; incorporation of, 62; houses, 62; trustees of, 62; teachers, 63; female school and teachers, 63; taken over by Pub. Sch. Soc., 63
African Sabbath School, 69
Aiken, So. Carolina, Colored School at, 70
Akerly, Dr. Sam., 125
All American Friends Conference, 201
Allen, Hervey, his *Israfel*, 151; his summary of religious conditions, 198
Almshouse, the, only home for Negro orphans, 64
Alsop, Thos., 74
American Archives, 75, 76
American Bible Society, Thos. Cock, V. P., 152
American Friends' Service, N. Y. Quakers' part in, 52; ment., 203
American Infant School Primer, by Mahlon Day, 124

American Medical Biographies, 134
Amity, the, of Black Ball Line, 153
Amsterdam, Classis of, 11
Andre, Major, 95
Andrews, Chas. C., hist. African Free Sch., 61; teacher therein, 61
Andrews, Mary, manumits a slave, 57
Samuel, signs address to Gov., 72
Anti-Slavery Society, use of cotton string by, 102; ment., 100
Appeals to Q. M. *re* m. intent., 90
Apprentice, status of, 55
Arbitration of disputes, 104, 105
Architecture, its present importance, 159
Arctic, the, lost at sea, Q. thereon, 124
Arcutt, John, teacher, 161
Arscot, John, teacher, 161
Assembly Journal, the, 60
Association for educating Negro men, 64
Astor, John Jacob, his work for Rob. Bowne; his silver watch, 33
Authors: Goold Brown; Chas. H. Bushong; Mahlon Day; Lindley Murray; Sarah S. Murray; Shadrach Ricketson; Valentine Seaman; Wm. R. Wagstaff; Sam. Whitehall; Jas. R. Wood; Sam. Wood

Baner, Dr. Llewellyn, 156
Baner, Wm. J., physician

Ward's Island Hosp.; m. out, 156
Bank of N. America, Q. in, 122
for Savings, the first, Q. prominent in, 125, 131
Mechanics and Traders, a Q. Pres., 137
Banks, difficulties of, relieved by Clearing House, 129
Barbados, Q. at, 8, 54, 146
Barrett, Walter, pseudonym of Joseph A. Scoville, 128, 135
Barton, Dr. Joshua L., his medical services; his philanthropies, 157
Barrow, John, V. M. Clerk, 139
W. H., in Pub. Sch. Soc., 181
Baton Rouge, La., colored Sch. at, 70
Baxter, Richard, his *Saint's Everlasting Rest,* 116
Beaman, Eben, freed his slaves, 59
Bell, Abraham, life member Soc. Ref. Juvenile Delinquents, 44
Bellevue, Lindley Murray's home, 121
Bellevue Hospital, 64; its development from almshouse to hospital, 154; Valentine Mott surgeon at, 150; Dr. J. L. Barton connected with, 157
Bedford, N. Y., law suit at, 159; Reformatory at, establishment of, 160
Beekman, Jas., his coach, 120
Beekman Street, shot tower on, 129
Bencker Street, 180
Benson, Robert, 75

INDEX 213

Bergh, Henry, his help in founding Soc. for Prev. Cruelty to Children, 50
Bible, 1st 4to in America, printed by Isaac Collins, 116; of Col. Orphan Asylum, saved by child, 68
Bible Sch., 202
Bickley, Wm., *et al*, get deed for land for Mtg. House, text, 207; plate, 30
Bingham, John, Inspector State Prison, 133
Birdsall, Mary, teacher in Frds. Sem., 173
    Susan, mem. Prison Assn., 45
    William, mem. Pub. Sch. Soc., 182
Bishopp, his *New England Judged*, 13
Black Ball Line, estab. of, 134; one of the liners, 1826 (plate), 134
Black Belt, the, Colored schools in, 70
Blackwell, Dr. Eliz. and Dr. Mary, their concern became a hospital, 51, 52
Blackwell's Island, 68
Bleecker, John, trustee African Free Sch., 62
    Leonard, a founder of Pub. Sch. Soc., 178; ment., 133
Bleecker Street, 37
Blind, Institute for, Sam. Wood helped estab., 125; R. I. Murray, Manager, 122
Bloomingdale Asylum, Eddy's pamphlet on, 119; ment., 118
Board of Education, Pub. Sch. Soc. work taken over by, 181
Boerum Place, Brooklyn, 38
Bogardus, Jos. A., merchant; orig. mem. Young Friends Aid Assn., 138
Bolter of flour, a, 73
Book of Martyrs, Fox's, large edition of, 125
Book of Records, lost and found, 57, 192
Books, for poor Negro children, bequest for, 60
Booksellers: Wm. Bradford; I. Collins; Mahlon Day; I. T. Hopper; Sam. Wood; Wm. Wood; Wm. H. S. Wood
"Bootlegging" in 1810, 85
Boston, banishment of Q. from, 8; martyrdom in, 8; whipping and imprisonment in, 12; bequest to poor of, 42; ment., 17
Bourne, Wm. O., his *Hist. Pub. Sch. Soc.*, 181
Bowden, Jas., his *History*, 155
Bowditch, Nathaniel, his *Navigation* used in Frds. Sch., 169
Bowery Savings Bank, Q. prominent in, 126, 131
Bowne, Amy, Y. M. Clerk, 141; in F. A., 177
    Caroline, in F. A., 177
    Daniel, 74, 81
    Elizabeth, Y. M. Clerk, 141; in F. A., 177
    George, Clerk Mtg. for Sufferings, 60; Y. M. Clerk, 139
    Hannah, wife of John, her service and death, 177

214 INDEX

Bowne, Hannah, in F. A., 177
James, 74
John, banished, 17, 21; gives land for burial ground at Flushing, 28; with John Rodman buys land for Flushing Mtg. House, 28; signs address to Gov., 72; Treasurer Queens County, 113; elected to Gen. Assembly, but would not take oath, 113; buys books of Bradford, 115; his descendant Mayor of N. Y., 145; his house, 190; ment., 30, 176
John L., in Pub. Sch. Soc., 181
Martha Joanna, her schooling, 161
Mary, signs m. cert., 206
Mary R., in F. A., 177
Robert, merchant, Astor beat skins in his store, 33; helped estab. African Sch., 62; inspector of State Prison, 133; descendants, 129, 136
Samuel, signs m. cert., 206; ment., 43, 81
Walter, Grand Sachem Tammany Soc., Senator, 116; the only Q. Mayor, 145; in Pub. Sch. Soc., 182
Willit, m. out, and retained, 90
Bradford, Eliz. (wife of the printer), signs m. cert., 206; ment., 115
William, printer, his map of N. Y., 31; Royal printer, disowned by Mtg., his place at Oyster Bay, 115
Bristol, Mary, Y. M. Clerk, 141

British army, occupies Mtg. House cellar, 78; auction of cribs, etc., at Mtg. House, 81
British Government, gratitude to, 79
Broad jump, a, 121
Brooklyn, Mtg. Houses in, 37; M. M. at, 185; P. M. at, 188
Brooklyn Hospital, R. K. Valentine physician to, 156
Brooke, Chas., 87
John, 161
Brown, Goold, his education, 122; his academy, 122, 168; one room thereof rented by Friends' Sch., 168; his *Grammar*, long in use, 107, 169; his *Grammar of Grammars*, 122
Jas., mem. Prison Assn., 45
Samuel, merchant, 73
Sarah H., 160
Buckley, Thos., in Pub. Sch. Soc., 182
Bull's Head Hotel, destruction of, in Draft riot, 66
Bunting, Chas. T., built Fifteenth St. Mtg. House, 36; portrait of, 36
Ella, mem. Wm.'s Prison Assn., 46
Burdsall, Ellwood, Y. M. Clerk, 140
Burgher rights in N. A., 9, 10
Burnyeat, John, his *Truth Exalted*, 20; held first meeting in N. Y., 20; ment., 190
Burial Ground, at Flushing, 28; on Liberty Place, 32; on

INDEX

Houston St., 175; removal of, 193; in Prospect Park, 195
Burling, Edward, his lot on Crown St., 30
— Edward, Y. M. Clerk, 139
— Elizabeth, in F. A., 177
— James, distiller, 73; disowned, 74; ment., 58
— Lancaster, joined Committee of Safety, 77
— John, Merchant, 73; ment., 81
— John, Miller, 73
— Samuel, attended concert, 95; struck a man, 105
— Thomas, took slave for debt, 58; disowned, 59
— Thomas, Trustee African Free Sch., 62
— William, in Pub. Sch. Soc., 182
Burling Slip, 146
Burlington, N. J., founding of, 9
Bushong, Dr. Chas. H., his work and services, 157
Bussing, Thomas, in Pub. Sch. Soc., 182
Business Meetings, their several functions, 186
Byrnes, Thomas S., in Red Star Line, 128; his death at sea, 135
Byrnes, Trimble & Co., established Red Star Line, 128, 135

Cambridge Journal of George Fox, 13
Calvinism, the cause of Dutch persecution, 18, 199
Calvinists, German, make theater into a church, 95
Camden, Delaware, 126
Camera Lucida, history to be seen as through, 39
Campbell, Patrick, 91
Cards, playing of, 95
Carle, John, Jr., trustee Bowery Savings Bank, 131
Carpenter, Benjamin, signs m. cert., 206
— Cynthia, Principal Frds. Institute, 172
— Henry, volunteer fireman, 136
— Jane W., Y. M. Clerk, 142
— Richard, Y. M. Clerk, 140
Castleton, Vt., Med. College of, 154
Catharine St., 35
Cemeteries. (*See Burial Grounds*)
Certificates of marriage, to be recorded, 86; example, 206
Chalkley, Thomas, signs m. cert., 206; his opinion of Ranters, 206
Chamber of Commerce, on site of first Mtg. House, 30, 32, 119; Q. prominent in, 119, 120, 128, 130
Chambers, Capt., whose tea was thrown overboard, 120
Chapman, Maria W., worked for equal rights, 143
Character, training of, 6
Charity Ball, compared with Q. philanthropy, 48
Chase, William Henry, 82
Chatham M. M., 160
Chatham St. Sch. No. 1 on, 180
Cheeseman, Dr. John C., surgeon N. Y. Hosp., 132, 149;

President Medical Soc., 149; ment., 152, 155
Dr. Timothy M., in Academy of Med., 149
Dr. Timothy M., Jr., professor in college of Phys. and Surg., 150
Child, Lydia M., her *Life of Isaac T. Hopper*, 63, 101
Children, not sinners, 6
Children's books, poor quality of, 125; Sam. Woods' little books, 125
Children's Court, the, 50
Children's rights, protected on widow's remarriage, 86
Cholera epidemic, M. M. raises money for relief in, 43; successful treatment by Dr. Wm. Seaman and Dr. Thos. Cock, 152
Christie St., 194
Christopher St. Ferry, 132
Christopher St. Subway station, plaque in, 132
Chronology, English and Dutch, difference, 11
Churches of N. Y. by Greenleaf, 32
City watch, Q. asked to take over entire, 79; willing to do their share, 80; numbers inadequate, 80; ment., 144, 170
Civil and Public Life, Q. in, 113
Civil War, the, freeing of Negroes by, 69; N. Y. Q. not much affected by, 82; Q. shot tower shut down during, 129
Civic duties, shirking of, 143. (See *Profit and Honor*)

Clapp, Benjamin, m. intent.; entangled with another young woman, not passed, 90
Isaac, H., in Pub. Sch. Soc., 182
John, in Soc. for reforming Juvenile Delinquents, 44; flour merchant, 137; Pres. Mechanics & Traders Bank, 137
Phebe, m. Richard H. Thomas, 137
Clark, Amy, in F. A., 177
Benjamin, in Pub. Sch. Soc., 182
Clark, ——, his *Astronomy* and *Penmanship* used in Frds. Sch., 169
Clarkson, Matthew, trustee African Free Sch., 62; a founder of Pub. Sch. Soc., 178, 179; ment., 62, 118; Thomas, his work for Negroes, 63; his *Portraiture of Q.*, 64
Clarkson Association, its mission for Negro women, 63
Classis of Amsterdam, letter to, *re* Q., 11
Clay, Henry, his cane, 154
Clement, James, an indentured servant, 54; his Ranterism, 23
Clinton, De Witt, in Pub. Sch. Soc., 180, 183; ment., 117
George, 62, 117
Coach, Robert Murray's, 120
Coal replaces wood as fuel, 168
Cobb, ——, *Spelling Book* used in Frds. Sch., 169
Cock-Cocks-Cox Genealogy, 152, 153

INDEX

Cock, James, 205
    James (of Jas.), m. cert., 205
    John, signs m. cert., 206
    Henry, signs m. cert., 206
    Sarah, signs m. cert., 206
    Dr. Thomas, in Soc. for reforming Juvenile Delinquents, 44; Physician in N. Y. Hosp., 132; success in Cholera epidemic, 152; award by City, 152; Pres. College Phys. and Surgeons, 152; V. P. Bible Soc., 152
    Thomas F., Phys. and trustee in N. Y. Hosp., 132; m. out, 153
Coenties Market, 163
Coenties Slip, 15
Coffee House Slip, Murray's wharf at, 120
Cogswell, James, founder and trustee African Free Sch., 62
Colden, Cadwallader, letter from, 133; ment., 117
College professors, Q., few, 159
Collins, Benjamin S., Mgr. House of Refuge, 45; in Pub. Sch. Soc., 182
    Charles, a founder of African Free Sch., 62; his antislavery attitude, 102
    Isaac, Mgr. House of Refuge, 45; in Soc. for reforming Juvenile Delinquents, 44; printer, his great care in printing Bible, 116; in Pub. Sch. Soc., 181; ment., 129
    Joseph B., in Pub. Sch. Soc., 181, 182
    Rebecca, m. Benj. Tatham, Jr., 129

Collins, Sarah, in F. A., 177
    Susan, in F. A., 177
    William B., his concern became the Traveler's Aid, 50
Colorado, Univ. of, Dr. Chas. Bushong elected to staff of, 157
Colored Home Hosp., now Lincoln Hosp., 157
Col. Orphan Asylum, origin and history of, 64; destruction of in Draft riots, 66; escape of children, 67; its present home, 68
Colored Mission, origin, 69; present home, 69
Columbia College, Valentine Mott, prof. of Surgery at, 150
Commandant, address to, *re* City watch, 79
Common Council, 116
Comly, Robert, dealt with for cutting wood for army, 78
Committee of Safety requests list of Q. 16 to 60, 75; reply thereto, 75
Comstock, Ann M., Y. M. Clerk, 141
    Nathan, in Pub. Sch. Soc., 182
Comstock, Elizabeth L., Life of, 82
Concerns of the Mtg., change of emphasis in, 39; not early adopted by Mtg., 40
Conclusion, 202
Coney Island Plank Road, cemetery on, 195
Conkling, Roscoe, 160
Conservatism, as to new matters, 40; a backward looking majority, 41

INDEX

Constant, Joseph, a founder of Pub. Sch. Soc., 178
Conscientious Objectors, in Civil War, 82; in World War, 83
Consolidated Gas Co., its occupancy of Mtg. House, 34
Continental currency, M. M. quotas to Y. M. paid in, 77; returned as "disagreeable," 78
Conversion, not sudden, but slow, 84
Cooledge, George F., publisher, his philanthropies, disowned, 123
William P., in Pub. Sch. Soc., 182
Cookery, peculiar, 79
Cooper, Sir Astley, 150
William, 81
Cornell, Edward, Y. M. Clerk, 140
Hannah, Y. M. Clerk, 141
Robert W., in Pub. Sch. Soc., 182
Cornwall M. M., cert. from, 135
Corse, Barney, leather merchant, 127; in Pub. Sch. Soc., 182
Israel, tanner; in Manumission Soc.; in House of Refuge; secured law against lotteries, 126; in Soc. for reforming Juvenile Delinquents, 44
Lydia, 127
County Medical Soc., 157
Courier, the, of Black Ball Line, 134
Cowperthwait, Elizabeth, her school in Flushing, 161
Grace, 161

Cowperthwait, Hugh, on com. to buy land in Jamaica, 38; bequeaths for poor of province, 43; ment., 161
Samuel, attended a play, 95
Crabb, Alice, of Oyster Bay, her slave to be freed by her daughter; land granted him by the Town, 57
Creek M. M., 149
Cresswell, Nicholas, his bitterness against Yankees and Q., 78; his *Diary*, 78
Cromwell, Richard, in Pub. Sch. Soc., 182
Crown St., Mtg. House on, cost of, 36; ment., 31

Day, Mahlon, in Soc. to reform Juvenile Delinquents, 44; Mgr. House of Refuge, 45; printer and bookseller, books printed by, 61, 172; his *Table* book used in Frds. Sch., 169; in Pub. Sch. Soc., 182; lost at sea, 124; his wife, in Wms. Prison Assn., 46
Day Nursery, Colored, 69
Deane, Daniel, m. out, retained a member, 89
Decision by majority, a sole case of, 101
Decker, John, Fire Chief, his efforts to save Col. Orphan Asylum, 66
Deed for land for first Mtg. House, text, 207; plate, 30
Delaplaine, Joseph, 81
Delavall, John, on com. to aid non-member, 43

Delaware, loss of, by the Dutch, 18
Demilt Dispensary, J. L. Barton Phys. to, 157
Descendants of John and Mary Palmer, 128
Dickinson, Hannah, m. intent., another man claims her promise; not passed; appealed, 90
Director-General Stuyvesant, his difficulties, 8; cause of his severity, 17; John Bowne's estimate of him, 18
Discipline, hard legality of, 98; known to few Q., 97; first printing, 98; damage and loss from its hard rigor, 149, 151; advice as to marriage, 88; as to profit or honor, 113; administration of, 97; dealings *re* I. T. Hopper, 99-102; now more liberal, 98; excellent advices of, 103
Disownments, for m. out, 74, 92; for military training, 74; for hiring substitute, 72; for not freeing slaves, 59, 60; of Valentine Mott, 151; of I. T. Hopper, 100; ment., 148
Disputes, peaceful settlement of, 71
Distraints for not training, 146; in Flushing, and Newtown, 74; in Jamaica, 38
Distiller, a Q., 73
Distressed prisoners, Soc. for relief of, 119
Distrust of Art, slowly outgrown, 95, 96

Divorce, almost unknown among Q., 87
Dobson, Mary, Y. M. Clerk, 140
  Sarah, care as to her cert., 91
  Thomas, merchant, 73, 81
Dock St. (now Pearl), 14, 163
Doctors, Q., 31, 146
Documentary Hist. N. Y., 73
Doudney, Richard, came on *Woodhouse*, 10
Doughty, Benjamin, 74
  Francis, 162
  Samuel, his slaves, 60
Downing, Phebe, Y. M. Clerk, 141
  Silas, Y. M. Clerk, 139
Downing St., Mtg. House on, sold, 37; P. M. at, 188
Draft Riots, destruction of buildings in, 65-68
Drama, unknown in Colony, 94
Drisius, Rev. Samuel, R. D. Minister, letter to Classis, 11, 12
Druggists: John B. Lawrence, R. I. Murray, David Sands
Duane, James, 62
Duane St., 180
Dunbar, Mary, in F. A., 177
Dungeon, the, its filth, 14
Dunlap, W. A., 117
Dutch, the, their settlement and system, 8; more humane than their officials, 15; English encroachments, 8
Dutch Reformed Church and clergymen, 9

Earliest Q. minute, plate, 190
East Houston St., cemetery on, 194; sold, 195

220　　INDEX

Ecclesiastical Records of N. Y., 12
Eddy, Ann, in F. A., 177
　Hannah, in F. A., 177
　John H., his map, 119
　Thomas, a founder of House of Refuge, 44; Mgr. thereof, 45; in African Free Sch., 62; in Humane Soc., 85; his report on drink and vice, 85; trustee Bank for Savings, 131; Pres. N. Y. Hosp., 131; *Acc't of the State Prison,* 132; Supt. of Prison, 133; value of his store, 136; Governor Bloomingdale Asylum, 118; pamphlet on insane, 119; *Life of,* 117-119; a founder of Pub. Sch. Soc., 178, 180; ment., 127, 164
　Thomas, Jr., in Soc. for reforming Juvenile Delinquents, 44; Mgr. House of Refuge, 45
Eddy, Sykes & Co., 117
Edgar, William, in Pub. Sch. Soc., 178
Edmundson, William, his *Journal,* 20
Education, 161; private tutors, 162; of children of former slaves, bequest for, 60
Electro-magnetism studied in Frds. Inst., 172
Eliot, W. G., Portraits of Physicians, 150
Elizabeth St., Sch. on, 34, 167, 169
Embree, Lawrence, in African Free Sch., 62; trustee thereof, 62
Emerson, Sarah H., in Wms. Prison Assn., 46
Emmett, Thomas A., trustee African Free Sch., 63
Employment office, Colored, 69
Employment Soc., 143
England, spread of Q. from, 8
English colonies, encroachments by, 18; persecution ended by, 18
Engineering, its present importance, 159
Ephesus, Matinecock compared to, 206
Episcopal Church, Q. joined, 135, 136; its Sch., 162
Equal rights, 51
Equal Suffrage, 51, 143; opposed by a few, 112
Equality of the sexes, 110
Erie Canal, Thos. Eddy's promotion of, 118; its traffic, 100; ment., 170
Errors, large, of Q., 113, 114
Euclid, geometry used in Frds. Sch., 169
Evans, John, companion to Burnyeat, 21; signs m. cert., 206
Evernghim, Abigail, Y. M. Clerk, 141 (m. Wm. R. Thurston)
Exemption from military service, 73; of Q. and firemen, 77
Executive Council, its action on Q. address, 72

Farmer (prob. Palmer), John, his concern *re* slavery, 56

INDEX 221

Farnham M. M., 157
Farrington, Samuel, neglects meeting for want of clothes, clothes furnished, 25
Thomas, 43
Fat sheep, payment for schooling, 161
Feake, Tobias, Schout of Flushing, banished, 16
  Elizabeth (wife of John), signs m. cert., 205, 206
  Elizabeth (dau. of John), signs m. cert., 206
  Hannah, her m. cert., 205
  John, signs address to Gov., 72; signs m. cert., 205, 206
  Mary, signs m. cert., 206
  Robert, signs m. cert., 206
Female Association, the, Sch. established by, 176; its members, 177; ment., 43, 142
Few, W., Inspector of State Prison, 133
Field, Caleb, 74
  Deborah M., Y. M. Clerk, 141
  John, his slaves, 59
  Mary Jane, Y. M. Clerk, 142
  Robert, signs m. cert., 206
  Robert, regrets dau. m. out, 90
  Thomas, neglects Mtg., 24
  William, shopkeeper, 73; m. out, 89
Fifth Avenue, unpaved, crossing laid for Col. Orphan Asylum, 65
Fifteenth Street, Mtg. House built, 35; on Stuyvesant's land, 18; M. M. at, 185; P. M. at, 187; a marriage at, 93
Fire, the $20,000,000
  buckets, by front door, 137
  and light, importance of, in N. A., 9, 10
  companies, volunteer, many Q. members, 136
Fireman's hat, compared to "plain" one, 137
Firewood, high price of, 168
First day Schools, early establishment of, 40; in Phila., 39; ment., 203
"First Publishers of Truth," 13, 20, 199
Fiscal, the, of N. A., 12
Flour business of N. Y., 100
Flour merchants: John Clapp, George F. White, Silas Wood
Flower Hospital, Dr. Chas. MacDowell lecturer at, 158
Flushing, spread of Q. in, 16; Governor's order against, 16; the protest, political effects of, 16; Town Meeting abolished, 17; Burnyeat at, 20; Mtg. House at, 28; distraints at, 74; occupied by British, 81; P. M. at, 81; First Sch. in the Town built by Q., 162; Female Assn. of, 183; ment., 30, 55, 90, 146, 147, 184, 207
Fort at N. Y., repair of, 71, 72; Q. not willing to help, 71
Foster, Miles, Mtg. at his house, 29; sold Keith's books, 29; chosen collector, but ineli-

gible as a Q., 114; ment., 42
Rebecca, bequest of Negro girl to, 42
Forster. (*See Foster*)
Foulke, Hugh, teacher in Frds. Sem., 173
Thomas, principal in Frds. Sem., 173
Fourth of July, a school day, 173
Fowler, Robert, his *Relation*, his voyage, 9; his visit to Stuyvesant, 11
Fox, George, parentage, 5; inspiration, 5; his ideal of education, 6; his *Journal*, 13; did not enter N. Y., 21; his attitude to slavery, 54; and to war, 71; his *Paper of Advice*, 97, 149, 198; the Inward Light, 198; his divine common sense, 198; tercentenary of his birth, 200; ment., 108, 110, 159
France, Q. in, 8
Francis, Samuel W., his *Sketches of Living Surgeons*, 151, 153
Franklin, Henry, neglects Mtg., 24
John, shopkeeper, 73
Maria, m. De Witt Clinton, 183
Matthew, bequest for Sch. books for children of former slaves, 60; in Pub. Sch. Soc., 182
Samuel, storekeeper, 74
Thomas, hatter and merchant, 73; Inspector of State Prison, 133; in Pub. Sch. Soc., 178
Walter, shopkeeper, 73
Freed slaves to be aided, 60
Fresh Pond Road (now Clermont Ave.), Maspeth, 37
Friendly Hand, the, history and work, 49; ment., 143
"Friendly language," of State Prison report, 133
Friends' Academy, Locust Valley, 138
Friends' Employment Soc., history and work, 47
Friends' grammar sch. in Phila., 117, 121, 164
Friends' Historical library, Swarthmore, 36
Friends in N. Y., by Wm. H. S. Wood, 126
Friends' Institute, Spartan simplicity in, 172; its principals, 172; ment., 124. (*See Friends' Sch.*)
Friends' Reference library, London, 166
Friends' School, on Pearl St., sold, 168; ment., 64, 153, 167
on Liberty St., established, 163
on Elizabeth St., 170; legacy from Robert Murray, 167; 7 at a desk, 172; rates in 1826, 171; Lancasterian system in, 168; No. of pupils and families, 168; rates inadequate, 167; letter to London for teacher, 164, 165
on Henry St., 174
on Orchard St., 174

INDEX

Friends' Seminary, established, 35; kindergarten in, 96; altered, 35, 174; on Stuyvesant's land, 18; teachers in, 157, 173; odd reasons for quitting, 173; no Q. child to be excluded, 174; ment., 156, 193
Frost, Gideon, founded Frds. Academy, 138
    Hannah M., Y. M. Clerk, 141
Fry, William, signs m. cert., 206
Fulton, Robert, 117
Fundamental law of Holland, transgressed by Stuyvesant, 16
Funerals, liquor to be no longer given at, 85

Garbage, thrown in gutter, 170
Gas Company, the first, house first lighted, 136; Hester St. Mtg. House long used by, 34
Gavan, Theresa, teacher in F. A. Sch., 176
General Assembly, its attempt to relieve Q. from oath, 114
Genesis, the, 8
Gerry, Elbridge T., in Soc. for preventing cruelty to children, 50
Gibbons, Abby H., in Wms. Prison Assn., 46
    James S., disowned, 100; in Pub. Sch. Soc., 182; ment., 99
    Sarah, came on *Woodhouse*, 10
Gilbert, William W., Inspector of State Prison, 133
Glazier, Lydia, 49

Goerck and Mangin, their map of N. Y., 31
Golden Rule Club, a live philanthropy, 52
Goodhue, Jonathan and Co., acquired Black Ball Line, 135
Goodrich, his Picture of N. Y., 33, 34
Good Samaritan, a, 15
Good will and esteem acquired, 144
Gould, Thomas, 165, 166
Government, cost of, willingly paid, but not preparation for war, 71
Governor, address to, 71; action thereon, 72; plate, 72
Grammar of Geography, by Jacob Willetts, 170
Grammarians, Q., Lindley Murray, Goold Brown, 107; their books, 122, 123
Grand Central Station, a Murray cornfield, 120
Gravesend, Q. in, 13; Burnyeat at, 20; M. M. held there, 184
Gravestones, objection to, 196
Greenleaf, his *History of N. Y. Churches*, 32, 33
Green Street (now Liberty Place), land bought on, 30, 31
Greenwich Street, State Prison on, 132
Greenwich village, P. M. at, 188
Greenwood Cemetery, 175
Griffen, Richard, 162
Grim, David, his map of N. Y., 30
Grinnell, Joseph, shipowner, 136

Griscom, David, Jr., principal Frds. Inst., 172
John, V. P. Soc. for reforming Juvenile Delinquents, 44
Grog shops, numerous, 170
Guest, John, Judge, deed acknowledged before, 210
Gummere, Francis B., 170
John, his *Surveying* used in Frds. Sch., 169
Samuel J., 169

Hague Street, 33
Hahneman Hospital, 138
Haines, Samuel B., 131
Haight, Mary, m. out, 87
Samuel, arbitration of a difference, 104
Hallett, Naomi, her light behavior, 91
Sarah, in F. A., 177
Hallock, James C., established N. Y. Clearing House, 129; ment., 49
Halsey, Anthony P., in Pub. Sch. Soc., 182
Hamilton, Alexander, 62
Hamlet, played in N. Y., 95
Harlem Railroad, horse drawn, 170
Harpas, William, 210
Harrison's Purchase, 157
Hat, worn in houses, but not during prayers, 24; Robert Fowler did not remove, before Governor, 11
Hatter, a Q., 73
Haverford College, 153
Haviland, Eben, 81
Robert S., Y. M. Clerk, 140
James S., Y. M. Clerk, 140

Haydock, Hannah, Y. M. Clerk, 141
Henry, merchant, 81; ment., 73
Mary B., in F. A., 177
Rebecca, in F. A., 177
Robert, trustee Bowery Savings Bank, 131
Robert H., trustee Bowery Savings Bank, 131
Hazard, Thomas, whaler, merchant, 137
Heart, Edward, Town Clerk, Flushing, 17
Hebrew Hospital, 151
Hedger, Thomas, drunk at court; ack. to be made public, 84; arbitration of difference, 104
Hedges, Stephen, 74
Hell Gate, 9
Hempstead, first Mtg. in province held in, 13
Henry Street, Mtg. on, 35; M. M. at, 185; P. M. at, 188
Henry and Clark Streets, Bkn., Mtg. House at, 37
Hester Street, Mtg. House on, 34, 35, 167; M. M. at, 185; P. M. at, 187
Hicks, Abigail, 129
Benjamin D., director Soc. for Prev. Cruelty to Children, 51
Elias, death mask of, trouble resulting therefrom, 36; on com. *re* accepting rent from army, 78; *Journal*, 78; ment., 129
Elias, Jr., ship chandler, 128; Pres. Chamber of Commerce, 128, 130

INDEX

Hicks, John D., trustee and Pres. Bowery Savings Bank, 131
— Mary U., Y. M. Clerk, 141
— Rachel, Y. M. Clerk, 142
— Samuel, merchant, in Red Star Line, 135; in Pub. Sch. Soc., 182
— Valentine, in Pub. Sch. Soc., 182; ment., 128, 129
— Willett, in Prison Assn., 45; "the Q. bishop," 103
"Hicksite" Friends, Mtg. House on 15th St., 35
High Point, S. Carolina, Colored Sch. at, 70
Hilyard, James, with bro. built 20th St. Mtg. House, 35
— Joseph, with bro. built 20th St. Mtg. House, 35
Hinsdale, Henry, in Pub. Sch. Soc., 182
"Hireling priest," a thing of the past, 87
History of Flushing, Waller's, 183
History of Pub. Sch. Soc., 121, 128, 181
History of Soc. of Frds., Wagstaff's, 155
Hitchin M. M., England, 129
Hodgson, Robert, came on *Woodhouse*, 10; visits Stuyvesant, 11; holds Mtg. in Hempstead, 13; imprisoned, 14; cruelly punished, 15
Holdgate, England, 121
Holland, Q. in, 8; ment., 23
Hollyoake, William, his antipathy to Q., 18
Holmes, Samuel, m. intent., 90
Home for Consumptives, 156

Homeopathic Med. College, 156, 158
Hooten, Elizabeth, first woman preacher, 110
Hopper, Isaac T., bookseller, in Prison Assn., 45; legacy to I. T. Hopper Home, 46; his *Life*, 63; his work for slaves, 63; trial, 99; appeal, 100; death, 101; descendants, 160
— John, in Prison Assn., 45
Horner, Isaac, Q. recorder, 189, 191
Hospitals, work of Employment Soc. for, 47
Houlding, ———, schoolmaster in Flushing, 161
House of Refuge, Q. Mgrs. of, 45, 122; Q. active in, 125, 127
Houston Street, sale of burial ground on, 201
"Housewives," made for wounded soldiers, 47
"Howard of America," the, Thos. Eddy, so called, 117, 132
Hoyt, Samuel, 162
Huddleston, William, 40, 209
Hull, Oliver, Y. M. Clerk, 139; ment., 81
— Penelope, in F. A., 177
— Wager, in Soc. for reforming Juvenile Delinquents, 44
Humane Society, report on liquor and vice in N. Y., 85
Humanity helpers, loss of some, 149
Hunter, Susannah, 90

Hussey, George F., in Pub. Sch. Soc., 182
Hutchinson, John W., in Prison Assn., 45

Iconography of Manhattan Island, 10, 31, 114
"If differences arise," 104
Impropriety of announcements at close of Mtg., 39
Inclenberg, now Murray Hill,

Indentured service, a means of emigration, 54
Indian affairs, Commissionership of, declined by a Q., 129
Indians, palisades to keep out, 9; Thos. Eddy's work among, 118; bequest by Lindley Murray for instruction of, 121; John Murray, Jr., active in welfare of, 180
Inebriate Asylum, 151
Infirmary for women and children, 51
In the olden Time, 120, 176
Intoxicants, 84
Ireland, spread of Q. to, 8
Irish servant, indentured, 54
Irving, Washington, his *Knickerbockers Hist.,* 18
Isaac T. Hopper Home, 45, 46
Israfel, 151, 198
Italian plasterer, an, his death mask of Elias Hicks, 36

Jackson, Anna M., her work for Negroes; Pres. Y. M. C. A.; advice sought by Police Comm'r, 143
William M., 139

Jacob Street, mineral spring on, 127
Jamaica, L. I., Q. in, 13; distraints in, 38; Wm. Penn at, 38; Mtg. House at, sold, 38; ment., 84
James Monroe, the, of Black Ball Line, 134
Jay, John, 62, 63, 117, 121
Jenner, Dr. Edward, his discovery of vaccination, 148
Solomon, teacher in Frds. Sch., 168
Jericho M. M., 151
Jerusalem, Q. in, 8
Johnston, Jane, in F. A., 117
John Street, theater on, 95
Joint Com. on Affiliated Service, 201
Joint Com. on Records, 193
Joint Y. M. 1928, 201, 203
Jones, Charles, Y. M. Clerk, 146
Dorcas (wife of Rich.), Mtg. at her house, 30
Richard, Mtg. at his house, 29
Sybil, 82
Journal of Gen. Assembly, 113
Justice of the Peace, m. by, 88
Juvenile Delinquents, Soc. for reforming, 44, 127; established House of Refuge, 44

Keese, John, 62
Keith, George, former Q., now agent of Episc. Soc., 29; Bradford prints his book, 115
Kent, James, 117
Kent, the, 9
Ketch, a 17th century, plate, 8
Kills, the, now Maspeth, 37

INDEX

Kindergarten, the, of Frds. Sem., 96
King, Hetty, in Col. Orphan Asylum, 65
Kirby, Edward, in Pub. Sch. Soc., 182
    Sarah L., in F. A., 177
Kirkpatrick, Daniel, arbitration of a difference, 104
Kissam, Benjamin, lawyer, 121
Knapp, Samuel L., his *Life of Thos. Eddy*, 117, 119, 178

Ladd, Caroline E., Y. M. Clerk, 141
Lafayette Avenue, Bkn., Mtg. House on, 38
Laing Industrial Sch., 70
Lancaster, Joseph, his monitorial system, his death, 175
Lancasterian System, used in Frds. Sch., 62
Language, help of Q. in preserving, 106
Lanier, ——, *A Century of Banking*, 170
Larson, Lars, Norwegian Q., his certificate, 49
Latham, Daniel, freed one slave, 60; ment., 74
Lawrence, Caleb, merchant, 73
    Daniel, ack. dispute with bro., 105
    Hannah, in F. A., 177
    John, in African Free Sch., 62; bolter, 73; ment., 81
    John B., druggist, 137
    Joseph, disowned for selling slave, 58
    Nathaniel, in African Free Sch., 62

Lawrence, Stephen, in dispute with brother, 105
    William, in African Free Sch., 62
Law suits avoided, 104, 105
Lawyer: Lindley Murray
Lawyers rare among Q., 159
Leather breeches, a common apparel, 6
Leather dealers: Barney and Israel Corse, Jonathan Thorne
Legacy to Mtg. by Rob. Murray, 34
Leggett, Thomas, 165
    Thomas, Jr., in Pub. Sch. Soc., 182
    Samuel F., in Soc. for reforming Juvenile Delinquents, 44; Pres. Gas Co., his house first lighted, 136
Legislature, address to *re* slave trade vessels, 61; act by, validating former Q. manumissions, 61; influence of Q. on, 118
Liberty Place (formerly Green St., then Walker St.), first Mtg House on, 30; Cemetery on, 193; ment., 31, 32
Liberty Street (formerly Crown St.), Mtg. House on, 31, 32; House sold, 36, 194; Frds. Sch. on, 163; M. M. at, 185; P. M. at, 187; ment., 32
Liberal Branch, the, called "Hicksite," 35
Libraries, at Mtg. Houses, 175
Life of Thos. Eddy, 133, 178
Life of Elizabeth L. Comstock, 82

Lincoln, Abraham, urged comm'rship of Indian Affairs on a Q., who declined, 129
Lincoln Hospital, the, 157
Lincrum, Mary, teacher in African Female Sch., 63
Liquor, no longer to be given at funerals, 85; progress from daily use to abstinence, 85; report on, by Humane Soc., 85
Literary Digest, the, 123
Live Oak School, 70
Livingston, Brockholst, in Pub. Sch. Soc., 178, 179
Lloyd, David, executor of Thos. Lloyd, 207
Thomas, deed from ex. of, 29
Locust Valley, Frds. Academy at, 138
London, England, music and pianos from, 33; bequest to Mtgs. in, 42
Lotteries, law against, secured by Q., 127
Lounsbury, Professor, 107
Lying-in Asylum, how established, 153

MacDowell, Dr. Charles, Pres. Academy of Med., 158; lecturer many years, 158
Macoun, Samuel, signs m. cert., 206
Macy, William H., Pres. N. Y. Hosp., 132; in Pub. Sch. Soc., 182
Madison Street (formerly Rose St.), Mtg. House on, 34; ment., 180
Ma   ncina, her concern, 49

Manhattanville, Mtg. House in, 34
Manual Bowery Savings Bank, 131
Manumission by Q., act validating, 61
Manumission Society, Sch. of, 181; Q. in, 122, 125, 127, 148, 180
Maps, by David Grimm, 30; by Wm. Bradford, 31; by Goerck and Mangin, 31; by Poppleton, 32; of Y. M. by Shadrach Ricketson, 149
Market Street, 35
Marriage, Q., barred in a will, 19; procedure in, 86; its simplicity, 92; engaged couple not to live in same house, 92; with wedding march, 93; legality of, established, 189
Marriage certificate, early, text, 205; plate, 206
Marriott, Charles, disowned with I. T. Hopper, 99, 100
Marrying out, disastrousness of disownments for, 87, 88, 153, 156
Marshall, Benjamin, in Black Ball Line, 134
Martin, Isaac, Tallow Chandler, 73
Mary Ellen, the cause of a new philanthropy, 51
Maryland, 20
Maspeth Avenue, 37
Maspeth Kills, Mtg. at, 185
Matinecock, Mtg. at, 190; m. at, 205; Ranters at, 206
Matlack, White, in African Free Sch., 62

INDEX

Matthews, Brander, 107
Mayor, a Q., 116
Mayor and Alderman, Court of, refuse office to a Q., 114
Means of Preserving Health, by Shadrach Ricketson, 149
Mechanics and Traders Bank, 137
Medical College, the, 150
Medical Profession, why it appealed to Q., 159
Medical Society, the, 152
Meeting for business, procedure, 40
Meeting for worship, basis of, 5; the center of Q. life, 22; first in the province, 13
Meeting in N. Y., at various houses, 29
Meeting House at Flushing, 28
Meeting House in N. Y., proposal to move house from Flushing, 30; built 1697, 31; plate, 32; sold, 32; 2d house, 31; 3d house, 32; on Crown (now Liberty) St., 34, 36; on Downing St., 37; on Queen St., 33, 34; on Hester St., 34, 35; used by Gas Co., 34; on Pearl St., cellar taken by troops, rent taken, but given back, 78; ment., 34; at Rose St., demolished by street opening, 34; cost of, 36; on 15th St., on Stuyvesant's land, 18; ment., 36; Y. M. raised part of cost, 37; on 20th St., 35; in Manhattanville, 34; on W. 27th St., 37
Meeting Houses, at Newtown, 37; 2d house, 37; at Flushing, 28; at Oyster Bay, 38
Meeting Houses in Brooklyn, at Henry and Clark Sts., 37; on Lafayette Ave., 38; on Schermerhorn St., 38
Megapolensis, Rev. Johannes, R. D. minister, letter to Classis, 11, 12
Members certified for exemption from military service, 73
Memorial History of N. Y., 148, 178
Memorial of Rob. Bowne Minturn, 136
Merchants, Q., list of, 73; Thos. Hazard, Sam. Hicks, John Murray, Jr., John T., Rob. R. and Sam. Willets
Mercantile Library, a Q. founder of, 126
Merritt, Anna, Y. M. Clerk, 141
  Nathaniel S., Y. M. Clerk, 140
Messengers, between men's and women's Mtgs., 35
Methodist Church, its objection to dancing, 95; ment., 116
Midwifery, Valentine Seaman's book on, 148
Military Service, in Civil War, leniently dealt with, 82
Miller, a Q., 73
Miller, Amanda K., Y. M. Clerk, 142; teacher in Frds. Sem., 173
  Joseph, imprisoned for refusing draft, 82
Mills, John, 209
Minturn, Benjamin, in Pub. Sch. Soc., 182
  Esther R., in F. A., 177

Minturn, M., in F. A., 177
  Robert Bowne, shipowner, joined Episc. church, 136; memorial of, 136
  Sarah Bowne, in F. A., 177
Minutes of the meeting, 23
Minveile, Gabriel, 146
Mission School, for colored women, 63
Mitchell, William F., in Colored mission, 69
Moderation and plainness, 108; present ideal of, 109
Molasses in cooking, 79
Monitorial system used in Frds. Sch., 168, 169
Monthly Meeting, the, origin and methods, 184; raises money for cholera victims, 43; not much affected by War of 1812, or by Civil War, 82
Moode, Eleanor, Y. M. Clerk, 140
Morality, low state of, 92
Morris, Lewis, Mtg. at his house, 29
Moses Brown School, 122, 170
Mott, Dr. Alexander B., Surgeon, 151
  Anne, Y. M. Clerk, 141
  James, Y. M. Clerk, 139; ment., 74
  Dr. Henry, 150
  Richard, Y. M. Clerk, 140; in Soc. for reforming Juvenile Delinquents, 44
  Robert F., in Soc. for reforming Juvenile Delinquents, 44; in Pub. Sch. Soc., 182
  Samuel, Y. M. Clerk, 140

Mott, Samuel C., in Pub. Sch. Soc., 182
  Samuel F., in Pub. Sch. Soc., 181, 182
  Dr. Valentine, surgeon, 132; remarkable career, his aid to Poe; Pres. Med. College, 150; in Soc. for reforming Juvenile Delinquents, 44; decorated by Sultan of Turkey, 150; ment., 152
  William F., in Soc. for reforming Juvenile Delinquents, 44; in Colored mission, 69
Mount Pleasant, S. Carolina, Colored Sch. at, 70
Mulberry Street, African Sch. on, 62
Mullenix, Horsman, his concern *re* slavery, 55
Murderkiln M. M., Del., 127
Murray, Catharine B., in Soc. for reforming Juvenile Delinquents, 44; Treasurer F. A., 176, 177
  David C., Sec. N. Y. Hosp., 132
  Elizabeth, in Col. Orphan Asylum, 64
  James, apothecary, appeals for bandage linen for wounded soldiers, 76
  John, in African Free Sch., 62; Pres. Chamber of Commerce, 120, 130; his fine trees felled, 120; value of his store, 136
  John, Jr., merchant, philanthropist, 122; V. P. Soc. for reforming Juvenile Delinquents, 44; in House of

INDEX

Refuge, 44; in African Free Sch., 62; trustee and treasurer thereof, 63; trustee Bank for Savings, 130; Inspector of State Prison, 133; Y. M. Clerk, 139; Pub. Sch. Soc. began in his house, 178-180; his death, memorial of, 63; ment., 117, 118, 164, 176
Lindley, grammarian, author, lawyer, in Soc. for reforming Juvenile Delinquents, 44; his *Reader* used in Frds. Sch., 169, 170; his *Grammar* long used, 107; his broad jump, 121; in Pub. Sch. Soc., 181, 182; ment., 81, 159
Mary (wife of Rob.), in Col. Orphan Asylum, 65, 84; entertained British officers while Gen. Putnam escaped, 120; in F. A., 177
Mary, in Frds. Anti-Slavery Soc., 69, 70
Robert, shopkeeper, 73; legacy to Mtg., 34; bequest for Negro Sch., 62; his firm, 119; his London coach, 119; his wharf, 120; in Chamber of Commerce, 130; legacy to Frds. Sch., 167; ment., 81
Robert I., in Soc. for reforming Juvenile Delinquents, 44; Mgr. House of Refuge, 45, 122; druggist, 122; Governor N. Y. Hosp., 122; in Institute for Blind, 122; ment., 64, 132

Murray, Robert L., in Colored mission, 69; Y. M. Clerk, 140
Sarah H., 120
Sarah S., *In the Olden Time*, 64, 69, 176; Sec. Col. Orphan Asylum, 66
Murray Hill, 120
Murray, Sanson and Co., 179
Murray's *Reader*, used in Frds. Sch., 169
Music, lack of, 6; and the drama, 94
Mutual Benefit Life Assn., 157

Nash, Francis, 74
National Cyclopedia of Am. Biography, 123, 151
Negro Slave, Hodgson beaten by a, 15; Mtg. helps member pay for one, 55; bequest for school for, 62
Negroes and Slavery, 42, 52, 54
Negroes, formerly owned by Q., bequest for education of their children, 60; great influx of, after Civil War, 69; Lindley Murray's bequest for their assistance, 121
Neglect of Mtg., how treated, 24
Nelson, James B., in Pub. Sch. Soc., 182
New Amsterdam, the *Woodhouse* at, 9; its palisades, 9; view of, 10; its one paved street, 10; alarm of its people, 12
Newark M. M., 185
New Bedford, Mass., shipowners from, 135

Newbold, George, in Pub. Sch. Soc., 182
New Chambers Street, Mtg. House demolished by its opening, 34
New England Judged, by George Bishop, 13
New England, whippings and martyrdoms in, 10
New faith, a, 5, 6
New Jersey Almanack, 116
New Jersey, a Q. Governor of, 113
Newport, R. I., 146, 147
New Rochelle, the "priest" at, 89
New Style chronology, 11
New Testament, used in Frds. Sch., 169
Newtown, Mtg. House at, 37; distraints in, 74; Q. at, 184; ment., 207
N. Y. Bible Society, Q. active in, 118, 126
N. Y. Clearing House, invented by a Q., 129
N. Y. Colored Mission, 158
N. Y. Exposition, used in Frds. Sch., 169; ment., 125
N. Y. Gazette, the, 33, 55, 115, 163
N. Y. Gazette and Gen. Advertiser, 24
N. Y. Gazette and Post Boy, 163
N. Y. Historical Society, 30, 62
N. Y. Hospital, first in City, 131; Q. active in, 122, 125, 128, 131, 153; ment., 118
N. Y. Infirmary for women and children, 138
N. Y. Post Boy, 76
N. Y. Preceptor, 125

N. Y. Primer, 125
N. Y. Public School, the, 161
N. Y. Spelling Book, 125
N. Y. Times, 107
N. Y. Wills, 18, 42, 60
Niles Register, 36
Nine Partners Boarding School, 123
Noble, William, dealt with for selling drink, 84
Norris, Isaac, a grantor for first deed, 207
North Gate of the City, 30
North Street (now E. Houston), cemetery on, 193
Norwegian Q., their ship and leader, 49
Nottingham, assize at, famous case at, 189
Number of Q. in City, 1671, 20; 1782, 80; 1918, 83; rapid increase of, 143, 144

Oak Street, 33
Old Merchants of N. Y., 127, 128, 135, 165
Old Style chronology, used by English, 11
Orchard Street, Mtg. House on, 35; M. M. at, 185
Ornaments, unnecessary, 5; lack of, 6
Orthodox Friends, Mtg. House on Orchard St., 35; on Henry St., 35; on 20th St., 35; in Bkn., 37
Osgood, Samuel, in Pub. Sch. Soc., 178, 179
Oskaloosa, Iowa, conference at, 201
Ostrander, M. W., in Colored mission, 69

INDEX

Oswego M. M., 149
Oyster Bay, L. I., Burnyeat at, 20; Mtg. House at, 28, 110; earliest Q. minute written at, 190; slaves manumitted early in, 57; Bradford's country place at, 115; Town Records of, 55, 57

Pacific, the, of Black Ball Line, 134
Packet ships, Black Ball Line, 134; Red Star Line, 128, 135; Independent, 134
Palisades of New Amsterdam, 9
Palmer, A. E., *The N. Y. Pub. School*, 161, 176
Palmer, Samuel, neglects Mtg., 24, 26
William, joiner, 73
Papists, Q. charged with being, 19
Parker, Dr. Willard, 155
Parsons, James, 74, 81
Samuel, Y. M. Clerk, 139
Pattison, James, commandant, exempt Q., from enrolment, 77
Peace and rest, felt in Frds. cemetery, 196
Peace and war, 71
Peale, Rembrandt, 148
Pearl Street (former Dock St.), Mtg. House on, 78; cemetery on, 193; Frds. Sch. on, 64, 153, 165, 167; Sch. house sold, 168; auction at, of army cribs, 81; cost of repair, 82; M. M. at, 185; P. M. at, 187; ment., 14, 34, 78

Pearsall, Elizabeth, in F. A., 177
Hannah, Y. M. Clerk, 141; in F. A., 177
Nathaniel, storekeeper, 74
Patrick Campbell, 92
Sarah, eloped, 91; disowned, 92
Thomas, storekeeper, 74; value of store, 136; elected to Gen. Assembly, but declined oath, 113; ment., 81, 92
Pearsall and Bowne, value of their store, 136
Peck Slip, Lindley Murray's jump over, 121
Penington, the, on Stuyvesant's land, 18
Penney, Norman, 166
Penn, William, at Jamaica, 4, 38; his settlers, 9; ment., 115
Penn's Library, 175
Pennsylvania, Q. government of, 113
Pension examining board, a Q. on, 157
Percy, Bishop, his *Reliques*, 94
Perkins, Charlotte, in F. A., 177
Benjamin D., in Pub. Sch. Soc., 182
Persecution, of Q., 17
"Peter the Headstrong," popular idea of Stuyvesant, 18
Petticoat, red, a payment for schooling, 161
Phebe Anna Thorne School at Bryn Mawr, 143
Philadelphia, Y. M. at, 78; Wm. Bradford printer at, 115; liquor licenses in, compared

234 INDEX

with N. Y., 85; Frds. Sch. in, 117, 121; ment., 99
Philanthropic meeting not allowed in Mtg. House, 99
Philanthropy, essence of Q., subjects change with years, 42; the second mile, 142; ment., 40, 42
Phillips, James, 166
Phillipse, Frederick, 146
Physicians and Surgeons, College of, 152, 154, 155, 157
Picture of N. Y., by Goodrich, 33, 34
Pigs, fattening in gutters, 170
Place of diversion, disownment for attending, 156
Plain dress, its origin, present conception of, 108
Plain Language, the, 7, 106
Plays, now given in Mtg. House, 96
Poe, Edgar Allan, helped by Valentine Mott, 151
Police Matron System, enactment prepared by a Q., 160; advice of Q. sought, 143
Police System, establishment of, 144
Politics, Q. in, 118, 127, 154
Poor Fund, the, 42
Population, in 1810, 85; our number compared with, 144; No. of Q. families, 168
Poppleton, map by, 32, 33
Portraiture of Quakerism, by Clarkson, 64
Portraits of noted physicians, 150
Post, Jotham, Inspector of State Prison, 133

Powell, Wilson M., in Soc. for preventing Cruelty to Children, 51; lawyer, 160
Rachel, in Wms. Prison Assn., 46
Sarah H., in Wms. Prison Assn., 46
Power of Religion on the Mind, the, by Lindley Murray, its many editions, 121
Prayer, hats not worn during, 24; rising and turning during, 24
Preaching, deterrent advice to young speakers, 40
Preparative Meetings, origin and locations, 187
Present possibilities, 203
Preserved Fish, shipowner, 136
Preston Patrick, England, 12
Prevention of Pauperism, Soc. for, 44; House of Refuge founded by, 44; Q. active in, 119, 125. (*See Soc. for reforming Juvenile Delinquents*)
Prevention of Cruelty to Animals, Soc. for, 50
Prevention of Cruelty to Children, Soc. for., history and work, 50; Q. directors of, 51
Printers, Q.: Wm. Bradford, Isaac Collins, Mahlon Day, I. T. Hopper, Sam. Wood
Prior, Edmund, value of his store, 136; Y. M. Clerk, 139; ment., 165
Edward H., his concern became the Traveler's Aid, 50

INDEX 235

Prior, Mary, signs m. cert., 206
Matthew, signed address to Governor, 72
Prison Association of N. Y., Q. members of, 45; Female dep't. of, 45; legal work of, 46
Prison Reform, Q. in, 46, 51, 180
Prisoners, distressed, Soc. for relief of, 119
Prize goods, not dealt in, 95
Profit or honor, posts of, advised against, 113; examples, 129, 144
Pronoun, plural, the, 7
Propagation of the Gospel, Soc. for, 29, 115
Prohibition, philanthropic work made easier by, 46
Property Committee, women on, 111
Prospect Park, cemetery in, 194, 195, 200
Providence, R. I., Moses Brown Sch. at, 122, 123
Provident Life and Trust Co., 158
Public School Society, the, established, 122; Q. active in, 122, 128, 181; members of, 181; ment., 43, 116
Public School System, origin of, 176
Public School, the N. Y., 176
Public School No. 1, established, 180; name suggested for, 181
Purchase M. M., 153
Puritanism, 199
Putnam, Gen. Israel, Mary Murray's aid to, 120

Quakerism, expansion of, after the Revolution, 144
Quakers, authors: Goold Brown, Isaac Collins, Thos. Eddy, Lindley Murray, Jacob Willetts; the "Raving,". 12; spread of, on L. I., 16; list of exempt, 73, 77; called hypocrites, 79; their help in preserving Saxon words and special meanings, 106; grammarians, Lindley Murray, Goold Brown, 167; intellectual cult of, felt to be behind that of other relig. societies, 118; a shot tower shut down during war, 129; their control of State Prison, 134; their schools, why different, 6; costume, origin and cause of fixation, 6; Increases and losses of, 88; numbers of, 144
"Quarterly Meeting trot," 35
Queen Street (now Pearl), Mtg. House on, 33; occupied by British, 81; cost of repairs, 82

Rabbi, Jewish, Q. doctrine by a, 23
Rahway, N. J., 91
Ranters, the, their lack of polity, 84, 89
Rare books, 192
"Rare specimen of a Q. preacher," 100
Reader, English, Murray's, 122
Reason why Q. cannot serve in war, 76
Record Room, the, 193
Records, the care of, by Wm.

Wood, 126; two sets of, since 1828, 193; ment., 189
Red Star Line, established by Q., 128, 135
Reformed Dutch Church, its opposition to Q., 12; land bought from, 34; its schools, 162
Refreshments, simple, of the Sewing Soc., 47
Relief Committee, the, 42
Relief of the sick poor, Soc. for (*See Female Assn.*), 176
Removal Certificates, 192
Renaissance, the, how begun, 202
Rent, low cost of, 165
Restaurationen, its passengers, 49
Revolutionary war, the, difficulties during, 75, 121
Rhode Island, a haven of liberty, 8; the *Woodhouse* sailed to, 11; the "sewer" of N. E., 12; Q. banished to, from N. Amsterdam, Hodgson went to, 16; Q. Governors of, 113
Richardson, John, signs address to Governor, 72
William, schooling of his children, 161, 162
Ricketson, Dr. Shadrach, Clerk of Creek M. M., 149; his book and map, and legacies, 149
Rickman, William, Clerk of Mtg. for Sufferings, 76; Clerk, 139
Riverdale, N. Y., present home of Col. Orphan Asylum, 68
Robbins, et, in F. A., 177
Robinson, Dr. ——, his former servant relieved by Mtg., 43, 147
Mary P., in F. A., 177
Sarah, in F. A., 177
Rochester M. M., cert. to, for Lars Larson, 49
Rodman, Dr. John, offers to move house from Flushing, 30; his lot on Green St., 30; land once his bought for Mtg. House, 31; on com. to buy land in Jamaica, 38; bequeaths 11 Negroes, 57; his distraints, 146; his wealth, 146; his services, 147; a grantee in first deed, 207; ment., 28, 55, 90, 162
Dr. John, Jr., his large estate, 147
Joseph, 43
Dr. Thomas, his ad. for runaway servant, 55; Clerk of N. E. Y. M., 147
Rodman Family Genealogy, 147
Rodman's Slip, 146
Rofe, George, his journey, his services in N. Amsterdam, 20
Roosevelt Hospital, a Q. trustee of, 128
Rose Street (now Madison), Mtg. House on, 34; cost of, 36; P. M. at, 187
Royal Gazette, the, 77
Ruptured and crippled, Soc. for, Q. V. P. of, 138
Rush, Dr. Benjamin, 85
Russell, Samuel, in Pub. Sch. Soc., 178
Rutgers Female Institute, 35
Rutgers College, 152

INDEX 237

Ryan, ———, his *Astronomy* and *Algebra* used in Frds. Sch., 169
Ryder, Hugh, shopkeeper, 73

Sadsbury M. M., Pa., 156
St. Augustine's Church, 193
St. George's Church, 73
St. John's Square, fine trees in, felled for R. R. terminal, 121
St. Luke's Hospital, 157
St. Vincent's Hospital, 151
Saintly lives, 145
Saints' Everlasting Rest, 116
Sanborn, Caroline V., in Wms. Prison Assn., 46
Sands, David, druggist, 137; teacher in Frds. Sch., 137, 174; in Pub. Sch. Soc., 182
Saratoga Spring waters, first analysis of, 148
Saxon words, still used by Q., 106
Schermerhorn St. Bkn., Mtg. House and Sch. on, 38
School. (*See Frds. Sch.*)
Schuyler, Philip, 118
Scofield School, the, 70, 138
Scotch Arms, Sch. opposite to, 163
Scotsman, a, former servant of, relieved by Mtg., 43
Scoville, Joseph A., his *Old Merchants of N. Y.*, 128, 135
Seaman, Jacob, trustee African Free Sch., 62
  Dr. James V., disowned for m. out, 148
  Dr. Valentine, in African Free Sch., 62; Surgeon N. Y. Hosp., 132; analyzed Saratoga waters, 148; introduced vaccination, 148; in Manumission Soc., 148; disowned, 148; ment., 149, 150, 151, 152
  Willet, trustee African Free Sch., 62., in Pub. Sch. Soc., 182
  Dr. William, his success in cholera, 151; in Pub. Sch. Soc., 182
Senator, a Q., 116
Separation of 1828, the, No. of Q. at, 144; causes of, 145; lawsuit after, 159; tragedy of, 198; ment., 7, 35, 88, 174
Sewel, William, his *History of Q.*, 116
Sewing School, Colored, 69
Sewing Society, the, 47
Sewers, absence of, 170
Sextant, the, lack of, 9
Shakespeare, his plays produced in N. Y., 94, 95
Shelton, Hannah, in F. A., 177
Ship builders: Lancaster Burling, Forman Cheeseman, Sidney Wright
Ship Chandler, Elias Hicks, Jr., 128
Ship of War, member dealt with for building, 77
Shipley, Ann, in F. A., 177
Ships, fined for carrying Q., 8; the *Kent*, 9; the *Welcome*, 9; the *Woodhouse*, 9
Shopkeepers, several Q., 73
Shot tower, a Q., shut down during war, 129

Shotwell, Anna H., in Col. Orphan Asylum, 64, 65
  Henry, 91
  Richard, ack. taking prisoners in N. J., 77
  William, in African Free Sch., 62; Sec. Chamber of Commerce, 130
Shupe, Walter, his philanthropic proposal, 48
Silver service, awarded by City, for services of Dr. Thos. Cock, 152
Simplicity, at funerals, 196; ment., 109
Sincerity, the bond of, 20
Sketches of Living Surgeons, 153
Slave, Mtg. helps member pay for, 42; bequest of one, 42
Slaveholding, disownments for, 59
Slavery, concern re 1717, 55-57; became repugnant to Q., 59; pro-slavery attitude of press, N. Y. Q. affected by, 99
Slaves, humane treatment of by Q., 59; freed as result of John Woolman's visit, 58
Slocum, Susannah, disowned for presenting forged cert., 90
  William T., in Pub. Sch. Soc., 182
Smallpox epidemic, 148
Smith, Elizabeth, signs m. cert., 206
  Hester, her defense of m. out, disowned, 88
  Joseph signs m. cert., 206
  Melancthon, trustee African Free Sch., 62

Smith, Sarah, m. intent., 90
Smith Street, Bkn., 38
Society for manumissions, 119
Society of Friends (official name). (*See under Q.*)
South Carolina, Q. Governor of, 113
Sowle, Andrew, printer in London, 115
  Elizabeth, m. Wm. Bradford, 115
Speller, English, the, by Lindley Murray, 122
Spicer, Samuel, signs address to Governor, 72
Spiritual loss suffered, 7
Stadt Huys, the, 14; plate, 14
Stamp act mob, the, 95
Standard Oil Trust, its Q. Sec., 138
Stansbury, Martha, in F. A., 177
State Farm for women, enactment for, 160
State Prison, the first, establishment of, 118; *account of,* by Thos. Eddy, 119, 132; cost of, 132; reports of, 133; historical plaque of, in Subway station, 132
States General, of Holland, law of, 16
Steam engine, studied in Frds. Inst., 172
Stevens, Dr. Alexander, 153
  Edward, *et al* get deed for first Mtg. House, 207; plate, 30
Stokes, J. N. Phelps, his *Iconography of Manhattan Island,* 10, 114
Storekeepers, Q., several, 74
Story, Patience (widow of

INDEX

Rob.), Mtg. at her house, 29; her m. and removal, 29
Robert, Mtg. at his house, 29
Stoutenburgh, Isaac, 118
Stuyvesant, Peter, Director-General, 8; his moderation, 11; imprisons Hodgson, 14; forbids entertainment of Q., 16; banishes John Bowne, 17; Bowne's estimate of him, 18; his later apology to Bowne, 18; ment., 144
Subway station, plaque of state prison in, 132
Sufferings of early Q., 16
Sultan of Turkey, decorates a Q., 150
Surgery, speed in, vital before anesthetics, 154
Swarthmore College, Sam. Willets endowed, 138; John T. Willets, Mgr., 138; ment., 156
Synagogue Anshi Chesed, 35

Taber, Augustus, in Colored mission, 69; Y. M. Clerk, 140
David S., trustee Bowery Savings Bank, 131
Tallman, Sarah, in F. A., 177
Tallow chandler, a Q., 73
Tammany Society, a Q. Grand Sachem of, 116
Tanner, William J., in Colored mission, 69
Tariff, or rates of duties, by Mahlon Day, used in Frds. Sch., 124
Tatham, Benjamin, Jr., his shot tower shut down during war, 129; declined office, 129
Tatum, Edward, in Colored mission, 69
Tea, thrown overboard by "Mohawks," 120
Teachers, Q., numerous, 159
Teaching, odd payments for, 161
Telner, Jacob, on com. to aid non-members, 43
Temperance, 51
Tenement houses, early, 180
Terence, Latin dramist, 71
Text books, in Frds. Sch., 169
Theater, the first in N. Y., its failure, 95; the 2d destroyed by mob, 95
Then and now, comparisons, 3, 14
Theocracies, the N. E. colonies were, 8
The Servant in the House, 96
Thomas, Allan Clapp, professor, Q. historian, 137
Phebe, 137
Richard Henry, 137
Thompson, Francis, in Soc. for reforming Juvenile Delinquents, 44; estab. Black Ball Line, 134, 135
Jeremiah, in Soc. for reforming Juvenile Delinquents, 44; estab. Black Ball Line, 134; large importer, 135; Clerk of M. M., 135; in Pub. Sch. Soc., 182
Thorburn, Grant, mail maker and seedsman, buys Liberty St. Mtg. House, 32; his

Forty Years in America, 32

Thorne, Anna M., Y. M. Clerk, 141
  Benjamin, disowned for being substitute, 72
  Jonathan, director Soc. for prev. cruelty to children, 51; leather dealer, 127; ment. 143
  John,
  Joseph, signs m. cert., 206
  Phebe Anna, her benefactions, 143; P. A. Thorne Sch. established by, 143
  Samuel, director Soc. for prev. cruelty to children, 51; ment., 74
  William, assisted couple to m. out; must ask forgiveness of bride's father, 89
Throat and Lung Hospital, Dr. J. L. Barton in, 157
Thurston, Abigail E., Y. M. Clerk, 141
  William, his Sch., 163
  William R., in Colored mission, 69; in Pub. Sch. Soc., 182
Tin roof, long life of a, 35
Titus, Edward, neglects Mtg., 24
  Hannah, signs m. cert., 206
  James, 74
  John, signs address to Governor, 72
  Samuel, signs m. cert., 206
  Stephen, 74
  William, attended play; dealt in prize goods, played cards, disowned, 95; ment., 74

Tobey, Dr., Clerk N. E. Y. M., 82
"Tom the Negro" manumitted by Mary Andrews, 57
Town Clerk of N. Y. (*i.e.*, City Clerk), Q. deed filed in his office, 30, 209
Town Meeting of Bkn., 195
Transplanted feudalist, a, 19
Travelers Aid Society, the, Q. origin, 49; its work, 50
Treatise on Surveying, by John Gummere, 169
Trimble, George T., his firm established Red Star Line, 128, 135; trustee and Pres. Pub. Sch. Soc., 128, 183; Governor and Pres. N. Y. Hosp., 128, 132; Y. M. Clerk, 128, 140
  Merritt, Pres. N. Y. Hosp., 132
Trinity Church, a Q. wears hat in, ordered out, 25
Truth Exalted, by Burnyeat, 20
Turpen, Lucy, teacher in African Female Sch., 63
Twelfth Street, Col. Orphan Home on, 64
Twentieth Street, present Mtg. House on, 35; M. M. at, 185; P. M. at, 188
Twenty Seventh Street, Mtg. House on, 48; P. M. at, 188
Two Weeks Meeting in London, letter to, for Sch. teacher, 164; reply, 165

Umbrella, a cotton, 182
Unanimity the rule in Q. Mtgs., 101

INDEX

Underhill, Amy, in F. A., 177
  Benjamin, ack. training, retained, 74
  Daniel, signs m. cert., 206
  Elizabeth U., in F. A., 177
  Ira S., in Pub. Sch. Soc., 182
  Isaac, 81
  James W., Mgr. House of Refuge, 45; in Pub. Sch. Soc., 182
  John, signs address to Governor, 72
  Joshua, in Pub. Sch. Soc., 182
  Joshua S., Mgr. House of Refuge, 45; in Pub. Sch. Soc., 182
  Mary S., in Wms. Prison Assn., 46
  Samuel, regrets being concerned in slave trade, 58
  Samuel, signs m. cert., 206
  Stephen, Y. M. Clerk, 140
  Walter, Mgr. House of Refuge, 45; in Soc. for reforming Juvenile Delinquents, 44; congressman, disowned, 117; in Pub. Sch. Soc., 182
Underground railroad, the, certain Q. houses stations on, 63; ment., 42, 54
Urquhart, John, teacher, his boarding Sch., 161, 162

Vaccination, discovery of, by Jenner; introduction in N. Y. by Valentine Seaman, 148
Valentine, Richard K., phys. to two Hosp., 156
Valentine's Manual, 136

Van Cortlandt, August, City Clerk, 74
Van Wyck, John, 74
Varick Street, 132

Wagstaff, Dr. Wm. R., his *Hist. of Soc. of Friends*, 155
Waistcoats, woollen, for soldiers, 76
Waldorf, Germany, 33
Walker, ——, his *Elocution* used in Frds. Sch., 169
  E. H., in F. A., 177
Walker Street (formerly Green St., now Liberty St.), 32, 35
Waller, ——, his *Hist. of Flushing*, 183
War, why Q. cannot kill, 71; Revolutionary, 75, 121; of 1812, N. Y. Q. not affected by, 82; Civil War, 82
Ward's Island, 156
Waring, Sarah, Y. M. Clerk, 141
Warner, George, Inspector of State Prison, 133
Washington, George, landed at Murray's wharf, 120; ment., 95
Washingtonian movement, the, 84
Watson, Jacob, 87
Watt, Agnes A., in F. A., 177
  Deborah Minturn, in F. A., 177
Watts, John, 118
Waugh, Dorothy, came on *Woodhouse*, 10; preached in street, 11; imprisoned, 12; banished to R. I., 13

Way, James, freed 3 slaves, disowned for not freeing others, 60; his bequest of land not accepted, 60
John (2 of this name), 74
John, Jr., m. out, 90
Wealth, acquisition of, some Q. weakened by, 143
Weare, N. H., 123
Weatherhead, Mary, came on *Woodhouse*, 10; preached in street, 11; imprisoned, 12; banished to R. I., 13; shot at sea, 13
Webster, Noah, his *Spelling Book*, 123
Welcome, the, 9, 115
Wessels, Matje, her inn, Mtg. held there by Edmundson, 21
West, Joseph, his bequest to poor of Boston, and Mtgs. in London, 42
Westbury, L. I., Y. M. held at, 78; Mtg. at, 190; cemetery at, removals to, 195, 201; ment., 152, 164
Westchester, Frds. at, 184
Western Inland Lock and Nav. Co., 118
West 27th St., Mtg. House on, 37
Whalers of Nantucket, 137
Whearley, Abraham, ack. drunkenness, 84
Wheelbarrow, Hodgson chained to, 15
Whitall, Dr. Samuel, chief surgeon Col. Orphan Home Hosp., 156
White, Edward, signs m. cert., 206

White, George F., flour merchant, preacher, his dislike of abolitionists, criticism of, 100
Whittier's, John G., *The Meeting*, 22
Willets, Edmund, in Pub. Sch. Soc., 182
Isaac, 105
John T., merchant, trustee Bowery Savings Bank, 131; Mgr. Swarthmore College, 137; Mgr. Soc. for Ruptured and Crippled, 137; treasurer of many organizations, 138
Maria, Y. M. Clerk, 141
Mary, neglected Mtg., 24
Robert R., merchant, 137
Samuel, director Soc. for prev. cruelty to children, 51
Samuel, merchant, in Manumission Soc., Pres. Soc. for prev. cruelty to children, 138; Y. M. Clerk, 140
Thomas, signs m. cert., 206
Willets and Co., 137, 138
Willetts, Jacob, his *Arithmetic* and *Geography* used in Frds. Sch., 169, 170
Williams, Sarah, neglect of Mtg., 24
William Street, African Sch. on, 62, 180
Willits, Richard, signs m. cert., 206
Thomas, signs m. cert., 206
William H., Y. M. Clerk, 140, 160
Willis, Anna M., Y. M. Clerk, 141
Anna W., Y. M. Clerk, 141

INDEX

Willis, Anne, Y. M. Clerk, 140
  Elizabeth U., Y. M. Clerk, 141
  Mary, signs m. cert., 206
  Samuel, Jr., 74
  William, signs m. cert., 206
  William, in Pub. Sch. Soc., 182
Wilkin, Robert J., Judge, 50
Wilmington, Del., 135
Wilson, James Grant, his *Memorial Hist. of N. Y.*, 148, 178
Woman's Infirmary, the, 153
Women, arrested for entertaining Q., 14; not in public eye as men are, 142
Women's Aid Society, 43
Women's Hospital, Q. phys. in, 151, 153
Women's Meetings, subordinate to men's, 110, 111
Women's Prison Association, their Home, 45; Q. members, 46
Wood, Arnold, 125
  Edward, Pres. Bowery Savings Bank, 131
  Elkanah, 153
  Dr. George B., 163
  James, Y. M. Clerk, 140
  Dr. James Rushmore, his remarkable services, popular clinics and museum, 153
  John, of Attercliffe, 125
  L. Hollingsworth, Y. M. Clerk, 140
  Mary, 153
  Samuel, author, printer, teacher, 124; Mgr. House of Refuge, 44, 45; in Pub. Sch. Soc., 182; his *N. Y. Expositor*, 169; ment., 135
  Sarah, matron, I. T. Hopper Home, 46
  Silas, flour merchant, owner in Red Star Line, joined Episc. Church, 135
  Stephen, Y. M. Clerk, 140
  Dr. Stephen, 156
  William, publisher, founder mercantile library, 125; Y. M. Clerk, 125, 140
  William H. S., publisher, Mgr. Bible Soc., director Y. M. C. A., his *Friends in N. Y.*, 126; Pres. Bowery Savings Bank, 126, 131
Wood's Almanac, 125
Wood's Museum, 155
Woodbridge, ———, his *Atlas* used in Frds. Sch., 169
Woodhouse, the, 9; its passengers, 10; Dutch account of, 11; bore no flag, 11
Woolman, John, his visit to L. I., his concern *re* Slavery, 58
World War, the, Q. in, 83
Wragg, James, his Sch., 163
Wright, Anthony, gave land for Mtg. House, 110
  Charles, in Soc. for reform of Juvenile Delinquents, 44
  Isaac, helped estab. Black Ball Line, 134
  Job, buys Indian lad, 55
  John D., a founder of Soc. for prev. cruelty to children, 50; Pres. thereof, 51; ment., 138
  J. Dunbar, director Soc. for prev. cruelty to children, 51

Wright, John Howard, Sec. Standard Oil Trust, Recorder for Mtg., 138
Mary, of Oyster Bay, liberates her slave, 57
Mary, in F. A., 177
Thomas, Y. M. Clerk, 140
William, in Soc. for reforming Juvenile Delinquents, 44

Yearly Meeting, its right in N. Y. Mtg. House, 36; Clerks of, 139

Yellow fever epidemic, Dr. Thos. Cock's service in, 152
Yeo, Emily P., Y. M. Clerk, 142
Young Child's A B C, by Sam. Wood, 125
Young Frds. Assn., 203
Young Frds. Aid Assn., history and work, 48; ment., 143
Young Frds. Movement, 201
Young Men's Christian Assn., a Q. director of, 126

Zouaves, the, protect Colored orphans in Draft riots, 68

www.ingramcontent.com/pod-product-compliance
Lightning Source LLC
Chambersburg PA
CBHW070728160426
43192CB00009B/1359